About Ray Barnett

Ray Barnett is the author of several non-fiction books including *The Gathering* and *Women In Christ*. As well as writing books, Ray's life has been a balance of many facets over many seasons: marketing management, advertising copywriting, pastoral work and Bible teaching. It has been a life shaped by a deepening understanding of the Kingdom of God and the necessity of seeing all of life as useful to the King.

While Australia has been his home base, and copywriting has helped put bread on the table, for most of the last twenty years he has been teaching the Bible to church leaders in emerging and oppressed nations. Ray and his wife Marilyn have been married for forty years, and have a growing tribe of grandchildren.

For more information about Ray or his other books go to **www.raybarnettbooks.com** or **www.littlemanbooks.com**.

Other books by Ray Barnett

The Gathering

Rethinking ministry roles for women in Christ

Revelation

A simple, powerful message of hope
for all believers,
of all generations.

Ray Barnett

Littleman Publishers

Littleman Publishing
www.littlemanbooks.com
info@littlemanbooks.com

First published, 2011

© 2011 Ray Barnett

All rights reserved. No part of this book may be reproduced in any form without written permission from Littleman Publishing except in the case of brief quotations in critical articles or reviews, or reasonable selections for study or discussion purposes.

All Scripture quotations, unless otherwise indicated, are taken from the THE HOLY BIBLE, NEW INTERNATIONAL VERSION®, NIV® Copyright © 1973, 1978, 1984, 2011 by Biblica, Inc. Used by permission. All rights reserved worldwide.

New Revised Standard Version Bible, copyright 1989, Division of Christian Education of the National Council of the Churches of Christ in the United States of America. Used by permission. All rights reserved.

Revised Standard Version of the Bible, copyright 1952 [2nd edition, 1971] by the Division of Christian Education of the National Council of the Churches of Christ in the United States of America. Used by permission. All rights reserved.

Cover design: N Blythe

ISBN: 978-0-9807440-5-7

Library of Congress Cataloging-in-Publication Data

Barnett, Ray.
Revelation : a simple, powerful message of hope / by Ray Barnett.
9780980744057 (pbk.)
1. Bible. N.T. Revelation--Commentaries 2. Bible. N.T. Revelation--Criticism, interpretation, etc
228.06

Contents

Introduction	1
Chapter 1: Keys to understanding Revelation	13
Chapter 2: An exercise in apocalyptic thinking	27
Chapter 3: Keys to understanding Revelation *continued*	35
Chapter 4: A story told in opposites	51
Chapter 5: Revelation chapter 1	57
Chapter 6: "I know your deeds . . ."	65
Chapter 7: The glory of the Lamb	93
Chapter 8: The scroll and its seals	103
Chapter 9: The Gospel at work	125
Chapter 10: Let the earth be warned! Part 1	139
Chapter 11: Let the earth be warned! Part 2	155
Chapter 12: The Son, the serpent and the saints	175
Chapter 13: The dragon's war	183
Chapter 14: The end of the rival kingdoms	197
Chapter 15: The seven last plagues	203

Chapter 16: The fall of Babylon   213

Chapter 17: The King rides to victory   225

Chapter 18: The end of the serpent   231

Chapter 19: Back to the beginning   247

A final word   255

Introduction

As it might have been . . .

Damon staggered along the alley, gasping for breath, his heart pounding in his ears. He vomited into the fetid pool that lay beside the alley wall, his body trying to rid itself of the terror he felt in every fibre of his being.

He had not been in the Colosseum, but even from half a mile away, he had smelled the blood as the screams of the dying had been submerged under an orgy of bestial laughter. Those sounds would never be erased from his mind. He spat bile as he tried to rid his mouth of the taste and smell of the dying.

He kicked the wall. He punched the crumbling stones until his fist bled. And then he sank to the ground, sobbing with uncontrollable anguish. He had wet himself with fear, and now the stains blended with his vomit and the filthy, back-alley puddle into which he had collapsed.

How long he lay there, semi-conscious, was hard to tell. His mind, delirious with fear and cold, raced with images of animals, swords, and the screams of the dying. In his delirium, he saw the face of Antonia, sweet and beautiful, radiant with the dreams of their future life together. He reached towards that beautiful face and as he did, it began to bleed. Huge strips of flesh fell from it, turning to sand. In his dream, he tried to cry out, screaming for the madness to stop, but a crowd pressed in on him, laughing and jeering, as Antonia's face finally dissolved into dust and blew away in the wind.

It was dark, very dark, when he felt the hand gently shake his shoulder. He awoke, tensed with fear, and would have lashed out with his fists if he'd had just one ounce of strength left. But every flicker of energy had drained out of him, and like Antonia's face, seemed to have blown away with the wind.

It was the gentle hand of Pontus. In the soft glow of the lamp in Pontus' hand, their eyes met. As if in answer to an unspoken question, Pontus whispered, "I know. Come . . ."

Damon could hardly account for the journey through the back streets of the city; his emotions had become almost as numb as his near-frozen hands and feet. They turned a corner and Pontus knocked three times on a narrow door. It opened, and just as quickly, locked behind them. In the dim light of the main room, a small group of familiar faces looked into his as he began to cry the long, deep sobs of the forsaken.

"I loved her. We were going to marry." His anguished words fought a losing battle with his uncontrollable sobbing. "Why? Why doesn't he stop it? You said he was the King . . ."

For Damon, the experience was new. For the others, it was a pain they had carried for a long time. Each had seen a friend or loved one dragged off to the arena to be torn apart by animals or used for gladiatorial target practice. They had smelled the acrid stench of burning friends drifting across the cold night air. Each had asked the same questions that Damon now asked, having lost his beloved Antonia to the bloody madness of the Colosseum.

"My dear little brother . . ." Pontus looked down on him with all the warmth of a father to a son. "Today you are weeping for Antonia. It was a painful journey for her, but her weeping has ceased." Not much else could be said.

It was some time before the youth was able to steady himself. They had cleaned him up and given him a warm, dry robe to wear. They were now gathered around the table, although clearly, appetites were not strong.

Once again, there was the secret knock on the door. It was Rufus, his face alive with suppressed excitement. Even before they could exchange their customary greetings, Rufus blurted out, "John has seen Jesus!" The room was stunned into silence. "It is true! We have received a letter from John on Patmos, and he has seen Jesus." Tears of joy streamed down his face.

"I don't think any of us has much strength left. I know it seems like the Romans are winning." Rufus gazed into their still incredulous faces. "But what I have here . . ." He paused, his voice caught in his throat. He tapped the letter, unable to speak, choking back raw emotion.

The small group was drawn inexorably into his excitement as they wondered where this was leading.

Rufus' voice was almost a whisper: "Jesus showed John the answers to so many of our questions, and he told him to write down the things he saw."

The atmosphere was tense with expectation. Rufus looked around at the haggard faces that filled the room. He looked at Damon, knowing just how painful it must have been for the new young brother to see his beloved Antonia hauled off to the arena. Each face he looked at was lined with grief and fear. Steadying his emotions with several deep breaths, Rufus unrolled the scroll and began to read:

> The revelation of Jesus Christ, which God gave him to show his servants what must soon take place. He made it known by sending his angel to his servant John, who testifies to everything he saw – that is, the word of God and the testimony of Jesus Christ. Blessed is the one who reads the words of this prophecy, and blessed are

those who hear it and take to heart what is written in it, because the time is near.

Even Damon's spirits began to lift as the words rekindled the certainties in his aching soul.

"Do not be afraid. I am the first and the last. I am the Living One; I was dead, and behold I am alive forever and ever! And I hold the keys of death . . ."

2000 years on . . .

As I am writing this, I have just left a room of men and women who live under intense persecution for the sake of the Gospel. Because of their love for Christ, they have lost what little they had. Most have been ostracised from their families. Some have been arrested; others have faced angry mobs. They live in a region where economic survival is all but impossible, their livelihoods having been stolen by successive political regimes, each of which has plundered the nation's natural resources.

We have just finished fifteen hours of systematic study through the book of Revelation. As our journey through Revelation proceeded, I watched the tears well in their eyes. Some said they wept all night, literally, for joy and wonder at the victory of the Lord Jesus Christ, and the certainty of their hope, as portrayed in this book we call Revelation. The book spoke to their hearts, healed their wounds, and eased their fears.

It is a wonderful book; a book of life and joy and refreshment. Indeed, I love this book.

More than once, I have taught and studied Revelation with persecuted believers in forbidden countries and seen it change their lives, strengthening their faith for the struggle with the empires in which they live. I have taught it to people for whom imprisonment, or even death, for the cause of Christ are pressing realities, and have seen God richly bless them with its message of strength and hope. That is why it was written!

Beyond all the voyeurism of Western believers who excitedly search the world's evil to find fulfilments of their latest prophetic theories on Revelation; beyond all the fantasy scenarios created by end-time novelists; beyond all the fear and confusion created by the spectacular and science-fiction-like interpretations given to the pages and events in this book, I want Revelation to be a blessing to you. Like all of Scripture, I want it to change your life by the "teaching, reproof, correction and training in righteousness"[1] it offers.

In that sense, it is no different from any other book of the Bible. It is intended for the encouraging, teaching, strengthening, and correcting of God's people. And yet it *is* unlike any other book because, more than any other, it is treated as a lucky dip of wild speculation, a hunting ground for every imaginable theory on the times in which people think they might live. Revelation has been used to make fools of believers again and again by men and women with an unhealthy fascination for evil, and who love to speculate on its embodiment in this president, this nation or that organisation.

I have seen people so afraid, that they will not even dial a phone number with the number 666 in it. A group of churches in one country in which I teach have buried enough food and water in the ground to last them seven years, and every few years they dig it up, use it, and bury fresh stores.

I have met people so confused by Revelation that they refuse to read it. For them, it is altogether too complex, too difficult. At the opposite end of the spectrum, there are people for whom Revelation has become almost an obsession. Every time you meet them, they tell you about some new computer called the beast, or

---

1   2 Timothy 3:16

a new microchip, or credit card, or world president or something that is now the certain fulfilment of part of their prophetic scheme. When each latest fad or fiction has blown over, they never seem to apologise to the people they have terrified or confused. No, they just leap onto the next bandwagon of speculation. I can't recall how many times over the last fifty years or so I have been told with overflowing excitement that someone has heard the Jews are about to build a new temple in Israel, or that there is a big computer in Europe called the Beast.

During my own lifetime, the book of Revelation has "revealed" various American presidents, Russian leaders and confederations of nations. We have been poised for a battle of Armageddon a score of times. Even when the calendar changed from 1999 to 2000, some Christians were driven to distraction by the fear that this would signal the supposed battle of Armageddon. And what fools they made of themselves and us all.

Worse than that, what fools they have made of Christ! A very dear friend of mine, an Indian Christian leader, tells of scores of terrified believers – pastors, in fact – crowding into his home at the turn of the century, uncertain of their faith and their future. That is not the ministry of Christ to his people! It was fear, fuelled and maintained by Revelation's myriad of end-time speculators and end-time fantasy novelists, as they portrayed a Jesus who cannot control his world, and a cross that cannot save them from a credit card or microchip.

As I hear some of the speculators, I fear that they have more confidence in Satan than in Christ, and certainly a far greater fascination with evil than with righteousness.

In some quarters, the interpretation of Revelation is a determiner of Christian orthodoxy or sincerity. One can disagree on many things in Scripture, weighing various opinions, but disagree on their interpretation of Revelation and they doubt whether you are even a Christian.

Is that what God intended? Did God think that his Word was too simple and so he decided to give us a blast at the end to confuse and terrify us? Did he intend to give us such a puzzle that only the super-students and prophetic magicians could interpret it? Did he intend to lock it up so that none of us could know what he was talking about? These are serious questions.

If our answer to those questions is no, and yet we find that people *are* afraid or confused, we are not reading or teaching the book as God intended. Or, dare I say, we are not actually reading the book at all.

A colleague of mine was responsible for marking a Bible correspondence course for a particular organisation. She discovered that she was at variance with the organisation's perspective on Revelation and so she asked the leaders if she was at liberty to answer students' questions according to her conscience. She was told that she would be dismissed from her position because she held a different view of Revelation from the leaders'. In a moment of inspiration, she had the temerity to ask them if they had actually studied the book of Revelation for themselves, systematically, from beginning to end. Their honest answer was no. This is a serious and yet fairly typical situation. Many people have a confirmed view, one that they will fight for and divide on, a view used as a demarcation line between sound and unsound believers, without having read or studied the book themselves. They have seen the charts and diagrams, read the novels, seen the movies, had their pulses quickened by talk of beastly computers, implantable micro-chips, and the latest rumours about the imminent commencement of a new temple in Israel, but have never actually read the book reflectively in its entirety. They come to the book and dip into it with a head *already* filled with all the fascinating, mystifying and exciting things they have been shown in complex charts or scary movies.

Exciting as they might be, popular novels about the end times are *not* Scripture. They are fantasy, pure and simple! They are fiction – hundreds of pages of the author's own creation, usually based on the tiniest hint or phrase from Scripture, or worse, based upon statements that were never actually in Scripture in the first place.

The pathway before us in this brief work is:

first to establish what it is we are looking at – what type of book Revelation is and what is God's intention.

second to work through Revelation systematically and simply, just as the very first readers would have done.

I do sincerely hope you learn to love the book of Revelation, to rejoice in it, to find nourishment for your soul in it. I hope it becomes for you one of God's green pastures in which you can lie down; a quiet stream from which you can drink. May it indeed restore your soul. May it become an abundant table for you in the presence of your enemy; wine to fill your cup to overflowing. Having learned to love the book, and the One about whom the book is written, may you never fear, even though you are called to walk through the valley of the shadow of death.

Fear not, little flock,
for it is your Father's good pleasure to
give you the kingdom.
Luke 12:32 (RSV)

ONE

Keys to understanding Revelation

Chapter 1

Keys to understanding Revelation

The interpretation of any piece of literature is determined by the type of literature it is. A fairy story is not history; a poem is not prose; history is not allegory and so on. What you determine a document to be – its style and structure – will affect your reading of it.

One of the books my middle daughter studied in her literature degree at university was Alice in Wonderland. Before reading it, the students were told it was Lewis Carroll's (Charles Dodgson's) scathing attack on organised religion and society in general. So, on that basis, students plunged into the book finding all sorts of allusions to historical personalities, events, places, and organisations. And indeed, if you have already decided that that is what Alice in Wonderland is about, you can certainly make it say all of those things and more. You can probably work out who each character is, what mushrooms and roses represent, or what jabberwocky is. However, if – as is the case – you accept that its original intent was a story written for a little girl, a story just for the fun of it without the usual heavy moralism of the time, you will read Alice differently. In fact, you will read it as the author intended, and you will probably thoroughly enjoy it.[2]

---

2   By way of interest, Lewis Carroll (a nom-de-plume for Charles Dodgson) wrote an Easter Greeting to his young readers of Alice, which was included at the end of the earlier editions, but not in most later editions – probably for being

The same is true of any kind of literature, including the various types of literature in the Bible. Psalms are not prose, parables are not psalms, the Gospels are not allegory. As we come to interpret any portion of Scripture, we need to approach it according to the type of literature that it is. In a parable, for example, the meaning is not in the detail but in the overall point of the story. In the parable of the Good Samaritan we are not required to try and work out whether the coins represent baptism and the Lord's Supper, whether the inn is the church, whether the donkey is the pastor, or the oil is a bucket of holy water at the entrance to a cathedral. To do so is ridiculous, and totally robs the story of its original purpose and impact. In the case of the Good Samaritan (Luke 10:25-37), a question was asked: "Who is my neighbour?" And an answer was given: "A certain man journeyed from Jerusalem to Jericho . . ." The meaning is not in the detail but in the story as a unit, because the whole story is the answer.

There is perhaps no portion of Scripture where the basic concepts of interpretation are abandoned more than the book of Revelation. The result has been that its message and impact have been lost in a sea of confusion and chaos. As we approach Revelation in this study, we will apply normal principles of interpretation. I have called them keys because they help us open its message. Please note that, while we are applying them to Revelation, they are the same sorts of procedures and interpretive disciplines that should apply to any portion of Scripture.

Key 1. The Style or Literary Genre

The book of Revelation is a specific style of Jewish literature. This cannot be overstressed. It is a recognisable, identifiable,

---

too religious. In it, he revealed his desire to show little children, brought up in the austere, joyless moralism of the time, that God created humour, wonder and imagination and that these things could be enjoyed without dishonouring God. He told his young readers that God had never intended their lives to be divided into two halves but that everything was to be enjoyed. Separate a document from the author's intent, and you can make it say whatever you wish.

unmistakable literary genre. It is *apocalyptic* literature. We find it in other portions of Scripture, however apocalyptic is a style not just confined to the Bible.

Apocalyptic is a style of writing that employs great images and symbols to convey truths that might not be readily discovered by normal investigation. Things from the spiritual realm, events behind the scenes, ideas beyond our finite understanding, are unveiled through great and overwhelming symbolism. Apocalyptic uses stars and angels, monsters and mountains, numbers great and small to convey the *feeling* or the *impact* of the truth even while the detail of the truth might be beyond human knowledge. As with parables, the message is *not* in the detail. Please underscore that in your mind – the message is not in the detail. It is not scientific literature with numbers that can be subjected to calculators and dimensions that translate into diagrams.

The message is in the overwhelming feelings and impressions conveyed through its images, and in the stark contrasts between good and evil.

Jewish writers were familiar with the concept of using huge, overwhelming images and hyperbole to speak to the heart about what God had done. Let's look at an example of this style of writing, one set in the midst of an historical book. In Judges chapter 5, Deborah is rejoicing over the victory God won for the people of Israel. Look at some of the things she said . . .

> "O LORD, when you went out from Seir, when you marched from the land of Edom, the earth shook, the heavens poured, the clouds poured down water . . . From the heavens the stars fought, from their courses they fought against Sisera." (Verses 4, 20)

None of us imagines that God has two legs and marched out of the land of Edom, treading so heavily on the ground that the earth shook. Nor do we imagine that Alpha Centauri or the Orion constellation fought for Israel. No, the stars and the constellations all stayed where they had always been, providing pinpoints of light in the night sky. So is Deborah lying? Is she delusional? No, she is overwhelmed with joy and unable to even begin to suggest what events or forces might have been at work behind the victory, so she speaks in huge images that match the abundance of her heart. The images are so strong that everyone around her is drawn into the excitement of the song. God marched through the land! The land shook! The stars themselves fought on our behalf! Rejoice!

Three thousand years later, we still understand what she was saying far more so than if she had given us a scientific and detailed description of the battle.

So it is with apocalyptic literature. The first readers of Revelation would not have searched for hidden meanings and details but would have taken the impressions, and the weight and impact of the symbols, and been moved by the enormity of what God was saying to them. It is when we try to find an exact meaning for every detail, or an interpretation for every symbol, that we get off track. We effectively deny the type of literature, and foolishness results.

Stepping outside the genre for interpretation leads not just to foolishness but to serious mistakes that can end up mocking Christ and robbing the people of God of his message for them.

Common mistakes when we forget the nature of the literature

MISTAKE: IT LEADS PEOPLE TO THINK THAT REVELATION IS ONLY ABOUT THE FUTURE

Forgetting the nature of the genre leads people to assume that the book is *only* about future events. The logic is simple: By assuming that all of the things described in Revelation are literal events, it becomes clear that we have not yet seen them. So if we haven't yet seen them, they *must* still be in the future.

However, consider some of the Old Testament images we read without so much as a second thought. In Jeremiah's day God told the people that he was going to send snakes through the land to devour them (Jeremiah 8:17). If we examine the historical record from Jeremiah's day until today, we do not see that event happening. So are the snakes a future event? Working the way some readers do with Revelation, we would have to say yes; one day in the future, snakes will come and eat all the people in Israel. And wouldn't we be foolish!

God's word through Jeremiah was an image of death; an image that drew upon Israel's history, taking their minds back to the time when snakes did come through the camp during the time of the exodus and death resulted (Numbers 11). Snakes did not come in Jeremiah's day, but death and destruction did in the form of the Babylonian army. God went beyond the detail, sending a message to their hearts with an image of painful, irreversible death. It was an image with which they were familiar, a reality drawn from their past. The image is powerful, even though there is absolutely no physical comparison or resemblance between Babylonian soldiers and snakes.

In Revelation, we are told about scorpions with hair like women, teeth of steel, etc. So some end-time speculators try to create realities that look like, sound like, and act like such things and they come up with Black Hawk helicopters or Harrier Jump Jets with long vapour trails that look like hair. And foolishness pours down like rain. Stick with the genre! It is apocalyptic literature. The message is not in the details but in the overwhelming impressions.

MISTAKE: REVELATION'S IMAGES MUST HAVE AN EQUIVALENT, IDENTIFIABLE REALITY BEHIND THEM.

In Revelation, we are told of the mark of the beast. In my lifetime it has been authoritatively declared to be bar codes, credit cards, social security numbers and now it is a microchip – something that can be put on our forehead and wrist. After all, that is what the Bible says. So the race is on to be the first interpreter to identify what the "mark" literally is, or will be.

In the Old Testament, God told his people that his Word should be bound as a frontlet between their eyes, and put on their wrists and the doorposts of their houses. Thinking literally, they made small wooden boxes, put copies of the Law inside them, and wore them on their wrists and foreheads. We laugh and say how foolish to make such a command literal. It is easy for us to recognise that, by doing so, they missed the whole point of what God was saying! How could they so misunderstand the *intent* of God? God was not speaking about words in little wooden boxes strapped to wrists and foreheads, but about his Law in their minds and hearts and homes. Everything they did and thought should be touched by the Law of God.

Might not ancient Israel now laugh at us as we scare ourselves with each new literal possibility? Is God's message to us that our eternal destiny is determined by a tattoo? Are we allowing ourselves to miss what God might be saying to us in the same way as Old Testament Israel missed the point?

Far more than foolishness, it becomes a major undermining of the Gospel. It sets the work of the cross against the ink of a tattoo. It makes the tattoo *stronger* than the cross, because the tattoo is capable of overturning the work of Jesus on our behalf. (We will think more about marks and mayhem when we get to that portion of Revelation.)

Revelation is apocalyptic literature employing symbols that go straight to the heart. They are symbols relevant to every generation and every culture, and they do not *have* to have a specific, literal, time-and-history equivalent behind them.

Mistake: Prophecy is always about the unknown future
Revelation claims to be a prophecy. For many, that word has come to be synonymous with telling the future, but that is not the way the Bible uses it. Prophecy may speak of future events or of past events, but it is a message for the present given to strengthen, encourage and edify the saints.

Our best definition of prophecy comes from 1 Corinthians 14:1-5. In that section, Paul is comparing the benefits of prophecy with the limitations of speaking in foreign languages to people who can't understand them. In verse 3, he says, ". . . everyone who prophesies speaks to men for their strengthening, encouragement and comfort." This is Paul's description of prophecy. It is simple, clear and direct. If you want to see prophecy in action, look at Acts 15. The Galatian churches had been thrown into confusion by false teachers, and we read that,

> Judas and Silas, who themselves were prophets, said much to encourage and strengthen the brothers. Acts 15:32

There you have prophecy in action.

The Old Testament prophets also took the Word of God and applied it to the current situation to strengthen, rebuke, correct, and encourage. They may have had a future component in their message, they also spoke of the history of the people, but their message was for "today". They spoke God's Word to the people in their day so that those people would be affected in their day, even by those things that were as yet to be fulfilled.

Mistake: Revelation's secrets are locked in behind mysterious, coded symbols
Another serious mistake that occurs when we forget the nature of the literature of Revelation, is that it is seen to be a book of symbols that only the specially gifted or initiated can master. This then

establishes an "end-times circuit" with these "specially gifted" people travelling from conference to conference, dazzling and frightening people with the latest speculations and fulfilments. But think about the nature of these apocalyptic symbols for a moment. Most of the symbols are universal. They are the images of dreams and nightmares: dragons, beasts, a hero on a white horse, a woman in distress, floods, falling stars, war, brides, thrones and harvest.

When we read of an angel taking his sickle and reaping the earth, we don't try to analyse the sickle or work out how big it must be to reap the entire earth with one sweep. Are we cut off at the knees or does the blade of the sickle slip below the soles of our shoes? We are schooled enough in images to know that a sickle is an instrument of harvest; it is as simple as that. Even a child can understand it. Even in the West, where we don't use sickles anymore, we still understand the symbol.

The light and colours of Revelation are also universal – red for bloodshed, light for goodness, darkness for evil. Heaven is high; its opposite is not just a pit but a bottomless pit – lower than the lowest. There does not need to be a literal pit that is "down", just as heaven is not literally a piece of geography that is "up". (After all, on a round earth, "up" for Australians is "down" for Russians and vice versa.)

Evil is like a prostitute; good is like a pure bride. Evil is destroyed in a banquet of blood and flesh, good is celebrated in a great wedding feast and so on. We understand these things. They are symbols that are universal and that don't need analysis or particularised identification.

Probably the best interpreters are children, because they don't try and make the symbols scientific or literal. Speak to them of dragons, earthquakes, floods and snakes and they take all the emotion of those images straight into their hearts and imaginations.

Revelation requires an ability to see the obvious, along with a child-like simplicity and receptivity. Adults compulsively complicate things to the point where they lie beyond normal comprehension. The purpose of the symbols is that they should be easily understood by all generations, in all cultures, in all of history. As the title of the book suggests, they are to reveal not to obscure.

However, a word of caution: to say that Revelation can be understood simply does not mean it is a simple book. As with *all* portions of Scripture, we need to reflect carefully on the message and its application.

We may need teachers to guide us, and we may need to stop and think for a while, but Revelation is not like the Greek mystery religions or Freemasonry, requiring secret knowledge held by a certain sect of the wise.

Revelation does not require major knowledge outside the Bible. It still has meaning for someone without CNN World News or the New York Times!

MISTAKE: EVERYTHING MUST BE LITERAL

It is by forgetting that it is apocalyptic literature, that people are drawn into our (particularly) Western desire to interpret every detail literally. Obviously, literal things do occur: there is a Christ, there is a Satan, there are enemies of Christ, there are martyrs, and so on. But those who try to make Revelation a literal book create enormous problems for themselves and everyone else because they are way out of line with the nature of the book. People will fight to the death over such things as a literal mark of the beast, a literal thousand-year reign on earth or a literal New Jerusalem descending from heaven. It must be interpreted literally, they say. But not a literal ten-horned beast, nor Jesus literally riding a horse with a sword in his mouth.

In fact, if we turn symbols into literal things, we have a remarkable Jesus! Jesus is a creature with four legs and a woolly jacket, he has seven eyes and seven horns, he sits on a white horse, and instead of a tongue, he has a sword in his mouth . . . Really? If we know anything about Jesus, we know that he is not a literal lamb! He was born of a virgin as a human being. But the term "lamb" is eternally powerful because it describes what his *role* was to be like – a sacrificial lamb. The word "lamb" is deeply and powerfully symbolic, but not literal.

We must be consistent then, in our treatment of the symbols. We do not feel we are being dismissive by not constructing a literal, woolly-skinned, four-legged Jesus with seven eyes. Nor are we being dismissive if we treat other symbols and images the same way. Look at what the image conveys about Jesus and rejoice. Then treat the other images in Revelation the same way. So much of the confusion caused by various treatments of this book arises when people step out of the literary genre and into literalism.

We should not be surprised if many different pictures or symbols speak of exactly the same thing. This is not a new concept for us. Ask Jesus what the Kingdom of Heaven is like, for example (Matthew 13). His answer will be that it is like a man sowing seeds in a field. It is like a mustard seed. It is like a net in the ocean. It is like yeast. It is like a pearl. It is like a treasure . . . Was Jesus confused? What is the relationship between a mustard bush and a pearl, or a net and a farmer? None, and yet each separate image or simile is speaking of exactly the same thing – the Kingdom of heaven. Why so many and such variety? Because each symbol adds another dimension to our understanding. In Revelation, Jesus can be a lamb, a lion, a horse rider, a man knocking at a door . . . Each image speaks of the same person but gives a different understanding of his character and function. Literalism creates enormous problems because literalism demands that each symbol describes something different.

No wonder a dear lady I spoke to in Russia said she no longer ever reads Revelation because it is just too confusing. What she had been taught was not only confusing, it was laughable.

SUMMARY:

The first major key to understanding the book is to know what type of literature it is and then to doggedly, deliberately, unswervingly stick to the interpretive principles that relate to that type of literature. Revelation is not history; not anecdote; not allegory; it is *apocalyptic*. Underscore that in your mind, because as a modern, rationally educated, non-Jewish reader, you will always want to drop back into the ways of reading that you are used to and whenever you do, you will begin to create things that are just not in the book.

TWO

An exercise in apocalyptic thinking

Chapter 2
An exercise in apocalyptic thinking

As people unused to reading apocalyptic images, we find it all too easy to step back into literal interpretations and applications. Just as we begin to get a handle on the major message of the book of Revelation, some well-meaning person will say to us, "You mean you don't believe in this or that? Don't you believe the Bible is to be taken literally? Aren't you just trying to spiritualise everything?"

So, let's get some practice reading images. The point of the exercise is to recognise how we *already* deal with apocalyptic images. We shall see the way God speaks to us through such images and the way he deals with our hearts and imaginations, and lifts our minds beyond what literal physical descriptions might do. (Please do the exercise, it is important.)

In 2 Samuel 22, David sings a song of praise to God for deliverance from all his enemies. He is overcome with gratitude, awe and wonder at the mighty hand of God that brought him deliverance.

Here are the words of King David:

> David sang to the LORD the words of this song when the LORD delivered him from the hand of all his enemies and from the hand of Saul.
>
> He said: "The LORD is my rock, my fortress and my deliverer;

my God is my rock, in whom I take refuge, my shield and the horn of my salvation.

He is my stronghold, my refuge and my saviour – from violent men you save me.

I call to the LORD, who is worthy of praise, and I am saved from my enemies.

The waves of death swirled about me; the torrents of destruction overwhelmed me.

The cords of the grave coiled around me; the snares of death confronted me.

In my distress I called to the LORD; I called out to my God. From his temple he heard my voice; my cry came to his ears.

The earth trembled and quaked, the foundations of the heavens shook; they trembled because he was angry.

Smoke rose from his nostrils; consuming fire came from his mouth, burning coals blazed out of it.

He parted the heavens and came down; dark clouds were under his feet.

He mounted the cherubim and flew; he soared on the wings of the wind.

He made darkness his canopy around him – the dark rain clouds of the sky.

Out of the brightness of his presence bolts of lightning blazed forth.

The LORD thundered from heaven; the voice of the Most High resounded.

He shot arrows and scattered the enemies; bolts of lightning and routed them.

The valleys of the sea were exposed and the foundations of the earth laid bare at the rebuke of the LORD, at the blast of breath from his nostrils.

He reached down from on high and took hold of me; he drew me out of deep waters.

He rescued me from my powerful enemy, from my foes, who were too strong for me.

They confronted me in the day of my disaster, but the LORD was my support.

He brought me out into a spacious place; he rescued me because he delighted in me. (Verses 1-20)

Let's interpret the passage two ways. The first will be literal.

From that prayer, try to compose a literal, physical description of God. Use David's statements and descriptions.

What the song is "literally" about

What we have is David in danger of death. His grave has cords attached to it and they are twirling out and around to try and catch him. But God acts.

God has a nose, and out of his nose he blows smoke. God has burning coals in his mouth and blows out fire when he is angry. God has feet and stands on dark clouds. He then gathers some of those rain clouds together and wraps himself in them, climbs onto the back of one of his cherubim and flies through the air. God is surrounded by darkness but is also so bright that lightning comes flying out of his presence.

God also has a bow and arrow. He shoots arrows at David's enemies and throws lightning at them. The fire coming out of God's mouth and nose was so bright that you could actually see the very bottom of the ocean and the foundation of the planet on which David lived. As it turns out, by this time David was in the ocean, and God, who has arms, reached down and lifted him out.

So the God of Israel has feet, arms, a mouth and nose, breathes fire, wears clouds, rides on the backs of angels while shooting arrows and throwing lightning at people, and is light and dark at the same time.

Is that the God you worship? Is that your image of the Eternal One? Of course not! But in saying so, doesn't that mean you are dismissing words from the Bible, treating what God's Word says as untrue? Again, of course not! We are clever enough to understand symbols and images. What is more, we don't even *try* to work out what the literal things are, or try to find the realities behind the images. In fact, most of those images do not relate to anything literal or real at all. By that, I mean that the fire in God's mouth doesn't mean the tail burner of an F-111, or that the lightning represents a line of tracer bullets. The cherubim on which he flew doesn't mean a B52 bomber, and the arrows are not nuclear missiles. But, of course that is *exactly* what some modern interpreters do with the images in Revelation!

Having seen that a literal interpretation does not work, we must now approach David's words as symbols and images, and to see what he meant by them. So, as a second exercise, read the passage again and try to write a simple sentence or two of what David was *really* saying about the events and about the God who rescued him. Let me show you what I wrote when I did that exercise . . .

What the song is *really* about

David was in extreme danger from his enemies and in great distress because of it. God entered into David's circumstances and fought on his behalf. Although invisible to human beings, God's awesome and mighty intervention in the battles could be seen in the results. When God fought for David, no one could stand against him. God's acts of judgement were complete and devastating.

The impossibility of literalism

Trying to work out what was literally behind each image David uses (in other words, what the smoke was, the fire, the coals, the rain clouds, etc) would be such a terrible distraction that it would cause you to miss the wonder of the message. And it would create a monster of a god, more akin to something from Hinduism than Yahweh as described in Scripture.

I once watched a panel of "experts" at a prophecy conference, discussing the latest things that seemed to parallel the images in Revelation. Some of those on the panel were men who had written the very books that had confused and terrified me as a young man. They each had a theory, and each pointed to this or that new piece of technology or new political alliance.[3]

Imagine those same men discussing David's song of deliverance. Yes, they would be just as foolish.

Having thought through an exercise like the one above, how would you answer someone who said that all of Scripture should be interpreted simply and literally? What would you say to someone who spent all of their time scouring newspapers to try and find something that might look like a mountain being thrown into the sea or a river turning to blood?

Revelation is apocalyptic literature. It is not coded information for the benefit of a select few experts, but a recognisable style of Jewish literature found in other portions of the Bible, as well as outside the Bible.

In the next chapter, we will look at the remaining five keys to understanding the book.

---

3   Their predictions and prophecies in those earlier books were *completely* wrong, but without apology they pressed on to make new predictions and speculations. Interestingly, because of the serious warnings in Scripture about false prophecies, and the stupidity and error of their earlier predictions, they were now deliberately saying, "This is not a prophecy, it is 'prophetic speculation'." Wonderful! What a brilliant escape clause. Change the word, and all is well. You can just keep right on terrifying or making fools of believers.

THREE

Keys to understanding
Revelation *continued* . . .

Chapter 3

Keys to understanding Revelation continued . . .

We have established that the first key to understanding Revelation is to clearly recognise the genre of the book. *Every* book fits into a genre or literary style. However, we need to go further. A document is not just written in a literary style; it will also have a structure developed by the author to help serve his or her purpose.

Key 2. The layout, or structure, of the book

As with any piece of literature, understanding the structure is important for helping us to understand the writer's intentions. As in most books of the Bible, structure is one of the most significant keys to interpretation.

I recall reading a biography, the first chapter of which described the funeral of the person whose story was being told. Then, in the second chapter, we were taken back to his birth, many years before. If I read that as a chronological account of events, I would be utterly confused. Was he born after he died? Is the book therefore about reincarnation? Or is the book about the son of the one who died, who just happens to have the same name, the same wife, the same children . . .? No, the writer of the biography had a structure in mind and felt it would be helpful for us to see the final chapter of the person's life and his effect on the people around him, before giving us the details of his birth, childhood and life. Structure is an important and significant part of the communication process. It adds to the impact and can increase our understanding of the writer's message.

It is a serious mistake to try and interpret Revelation without first determining if it has a structure other than straight linear progression. By way of comparison, John's other major writing, his Gospel, does not follow a linear chronological progression. In his Gospel, John uses a series of "sevens" to communicate what he wants us to know about Jesus. He selects seven miracles, seven teaching discourses, seven "I am" statements of Jesus, and lays them out for us in the order that best suits his purpose. In his Gospel, John has not written a chronological biography, but an essay on the life and work of Jesus of Nazareth that will prove to us, once and for all, that he is the long expected Christ, the Son of God. John places events and teaching in his own deliberate, chosen order to make his point clear.

So, too, with Revelation – it is a book of "sevens" and has a structure that is neither linear nor chronological. We have a prologue in which the hero and his victory are introduced; a prologue that shows us the first and second comings of Jesus, his death and glorification. Then we are shown the current (first century) circumstances of the churches to which it was written. After that brief glimpse of their circumstances on earth, we are taken back into heaven to see the central and total authority of Jesus as the conquering Lamb of God. Right from the beginning, we are shown different things at different levels, not a chronology of events.

This is most important to understand. It is actually quite easy to see this within the text of the book, but it has been all but smothered by the massive amount of speculative end-time material coming onto the market. The charts, diagrams, novels, and movies flood our minds until we are almost beyond being able to approach the book itself as a simple document, a piece of literature, whose structure will be revealed to us if we read it thoughtfully.

With the biography I mentioned above, I was a few paragraphs into the second chapter before I realised that I was now going back into the past, prior to the funeral about which I had just read. I soon discovered that there was a non-chronological structure to those few chapters, and I was not in the least bit confused. However, if a Hindu reincarnationist had got hold of the biography, with that theory firmly set in his mind, he might see the funeral as the first event, and the birth as the next linear event in an endless cycle of reincarnation. If, with that theory firmly in his mind, he made movies, wrote study guides and novels, and drew charts and diagrams about it, I would probably never have seen the book's structure for what it was. By first imposing his system of interpretation, he would then have seen the book as confirming the very system he had imposed upon it.

Let me say quite strongly that the chronological approach to Revelation may look good in the charts and diagrams but simply does not work in the text of the book itself. Let me give you just one example.

Look at chapter 6:12-17.

> I watched as he opened the sixth seal. There was a great earthquake. The sun turned black like sackcloth made of goat hair, the whole moon turned blood red, and the stars in the sky fell to earth, as late figs drop from a fig-tree when shaken by a strong wind.
>
> The sky receded like a scroll, rolling up, and every mountain and island was removed from its place.
>
> Then the kings of the earth, the princes, the generals, the rich, the mighty, and every slave and every free man hid in caves and among the rocks of the mountains.

They called to the mountains and the rocks, "Fall on us and hide us from the face of him who sits on the throne and from the wrath of the Lamb! For the great day of their wrath has come, and who can stand?"

It does not take much skill to work out what we are being shown. Every person on earth, from every level of society – kings, slaves, free people – *everyone* has seen God the Father and the exalted Lord Jesus. We are told plainly and forcefully that "the great day of their wrath has come" (verse 17). The earth's islands and mountains are all removed from their places. There is no sky anymore; the stars are gone. What we are reading about is the end. The day of wrath has come! And we are only in chapter 6! That alone should begin to awaken in us the idea that perhaps it is not a linear chronological document. But let's go further.

A few sentences later, in chapter 7:3, we read:

"Do not harm the land or the sea or the trees until we put a seal on the foreheads of the servants of our God."

God declares that the earth is *not* to be harmed until the servants of God are sealed. But in chapter 6:12-17, we have already read that the earth *is* harmed. So, does chapter 7 come before or after chapter 6? It is a simple question of literary analysis with a simple literary answer. The document itself shows us that the events of chapter 7 must happen before, or during, the events at the end of chapter 6.

It is an extremely significant point. From this, we begin to see that Revelation is not a book in which one thing happens after another in the flow and sequence of chapters, but like that biography I mentioned earlier, it has a deliberate structure. Events are shown to us out of sequence in order to make a point or to emphasise something. This is normal literary practice!

But let's go further. In chapter 16:20, we read, "Every island fled away and the mountains could not be found."

We have already read about that in chapter 6:14, "Every mountain and island was removed from its place."

So when does chapter 16 occur? Unless the islands flee away and the mountains disappear twice, it must happen at the same time as the latter part of chapter 6. Chapters 16 and 6 are parallel passages, each covering the same period of time and each taking us to the end of the world as we know it. However, as we shall see when we come to analyse them, each retelling of the events has a different focus. A different point is being made.

In fact, as has been ably shown in many good commentaries, Revelation is a series of overlaid visions, each covering the same period of time and each bringing us through to the end of history. (I hope you begin to see that working out in practice as we look at the text of the book.)

But doesn't John tell us what happens next, and next and next? All too often we read what we think is there, not what is actually there. This especially happens when we already have a theory that we bring to the text. If you look at chapter 7:1, for example, you read a phrase that is almost always misread. John says, "*After this I saw* four angels standing at the four corners of the earth [emphasis mine]." Those specific words are important! He does *not* say, "The next thing that happened was . . ." He tells us what he *saw* next. They are two very different expressions and radically change our reading of the book.

In his vision, John is not shown everything at once but is shown many things in their turn. Throughout the book, he is shown what happens to believers, to unbelievers, to the earth and to the kingdoms of this world. He is shown what happens to Satan and his angels. And each time, John reveals to us what he *saw next*. Each vision he saw, each major and minor drama, was part of the war between God and the kingdom of darkness, being played out on the earth and in the heavens. Each drama leads us through history until the end.

I recall walking through the Rijksmuseum, a huge museum and art gallery in Amsterdam. I had heard that Rembrandt's great painting, The Night Watch, was displayed there, and having never seen it before, I had no idea what I was going to experience. I reached the correct floor, turned into the gallery and was suddenly stopped in my tracks. At the end of the gallery, perhaps forty metres away, was an enormous painting, over three and a half metres high and almost four and a half metres long. It was magnificent; it was complex; multifaceted; with many characters, each with their own facial expression and demeanour contributing to the overall impression. The figures almost moved on the canvas. It is awesome to imagine someone putting paint onto canvas to create it.

Were I to describe my *experience* of that event, I would have to do it in parts. "The first thing I saw was the group of faces, lit almost as if by floodlight, in the centre left of the painting. The next things that caught my eye were the characters at the back of the group. As I drew closer, the next thing I saw was the detail of their clothing. Then I saw . . ." There is no way in the world I could give you one sentence to convey the detail or the impact of all that I saw.

In his isolation on Patmos, John is being shown the great drama of heaven and earth intersecting in the salvation and judgement of mankind, based on the completed work of Christ on the cross. He could not possibly give it all at once. Neither was he shown it all at once. He tells us the next thing he saw, and the next thing. My description of Rembrandt's painting would bear no relationship whatever to the timeline of the painting being completed, or the sequence of the events portrayed in the painting. I could only absorb it in parts and describe it the same way. So, too, with John's revelation. It is not a sequence of events related to time, but is overlaid descriptions of the highest and lowest, the greatest and least, the major and the minor parts of the fulfilment of the eternal purposes of God through the victory of Jesus. Each scene answers another question and satisfies our hearts. Is the world out of control? Why is history like it is? Why are believers being persecuted? What happens to Satan? Layer after layer of information is overlaid one upon the other, to give us the complete picture. It is wonderful! It is beyond human wisdom! It is given to us in images that themselves defy detailed analysis. But the impression remains – the joy, the wonder, and the excitement of the victory of Jesus. It is a book for the heart.

Key 3. The theme and setting of the book

Revelation was most likely written late in John's life. By then, the church had seen all the types of difficulties that would happen throughout history. They knew Satan as their enemy and could see his work in many different ways, just as Jesus and the apostles had warned them. They had experienced persecution on a large scale, both at the hands of Romans and the Jewish religious leaders. Satan, their great enemy, had worked through both the secular government and the religious systems to try and destroy them. They had experienced problems within the churches as false teachers – "wolves in sheep's clothing" – had risen among them. They had seen false religions and cults try and destroy them. They had suffered loss and pain.

As they saw their loved ones put to death as martyrs, it may have seemed as if the enemy was winning and Jesus was losing. It may have seemed, at times, as if Jesus' victory was not complete, that they were on the losing side rather than the winning side. The message of this book was given to show them that the victory is theirs *because* the victory already belongs to Jesus. Jesus *is* the victor. God *is* sovereign, and Jesus *is* his anointed king. It was a message to give them strength in the battle *then*. Consequently, it is also a book of encouragement and victory for all believers throughout history.

That the victory of Christ is the major theme and setting for the book is plain. The book begins with a vision of the exalted Lord, Jesus Christ who has redeemed men and women for himself. It shows him as the First and the Last, the one who himself holds the keys of death and hell. *He* is the authority, not Satan. No matter what happens on earth, or what things may look like on the surface, Jesus is the victor. The victory of Christ is not future but past, present and future. Revelation is a book looking not *to* victory but *from* victory. That is so important to understanding this book.

Any interpretation of this book that puts the victory into the future goes against the grammar and theology of the book. Look at the language of the early sections of the book:

Chapter 1:5 "Jesus Christ, who is the faithful witness, the firstborn from the dead, and the ruler of the kings of the earth." Jesus rules over the kings of the earth *now*!

Chapter 3:21 "To him who overcomes, I will give the right to sit with me on my throne, just as I overcame and sat down with my Father on his throne." Jesus conquered in the past. It is already done! He is on the throne *now*.

Chapter 5:5 "The Lion of the tribe of Judah has conquered." When did he conquer? In the past, on the cross.

Colossians 2:15 tells us that God "disarmed the powers and authorities, he made a public spectacle of them, triumphing over them by the cross." That is where death was conquered; that is where Satan's hold on mankind was broken; that is where the strong man was bound; that is where the Kingdom of God received its King. He ascended to the right hand of the Father and will reign until all his enemies are made a stool for his feet. Note that he is not waiting until they are made a stool for his feet before he can reign, he is reigning now. And one day, in his timing, he will make his enemies a stool for his feet.

And isn't that consistent with his words to those who watched him ascend into heaven, "All authority in heaven and on earth has been given to me . . ." (Matthew 28:18)? It happened at his first coming through his obedience unto death, and his defeat of death itself.

That brings us to the next key.

Key 4. First Century relevance

The book of Revelation is no different from any other book, in that it had an initial group of readers or hearers. And, as with any book of the Bible, correct interpretation begins with establishing what it meant to those first readers. In this case, it is a first century book, with a first century readership in seven specified churches throughout Asia. It was certainly written to be helpful to all believers of all ages of the church, as were the letters to the Colossians, Philippians, Hebrews, Thessalonians and so on. But, as with those letters, there was a first group who heard Revelation in *their* setting, with *their* problems and joys and fears.

So, while it does have a meaning for us and gives strength to us, whether we are in the last generation or not, it was *first* helpful to its first-century audience. They would need to have understood the message because it was a letter, a very long letter, but nonetheless a letter written to be read out loud to the churches of the day. God would not have written them an unintelligible, incomprehensible porridge of mysteries!

Consider how the letter begins: "John, to the seven churches in the province of Asia." (Chapter 1:4)

The churches were as real as the churches in Galatia, Rome and Philippi. We must take that first century relevance seriously. Any interpretation or application we make that would have been beyond the wildest imagination of first century Asian believers must be highly suspect!

Why did John write to *those* churches? Because he was told to. Is that too difficult? In chapter 1:11, it is simple and clear: "Write what you see and send it to the seven churches."

There is no mystery to it, any more than there is a mystery to the Apostle Peter writing, "Peter . . . to God's elect . . . throughout Pontus, Galatia, Cappadocia, Asia and Bythinia . . ." (1 Peter 1:1). No one reads that introduction to 1 Peter and makes deep mysterious meanings from it. No one suggests that Peter is writing to various ages of church history under coded names. Peter's words are accepted for what they are. If the Holy Spirit decided to have Peter write to those specific churches, he is most welcome to do so. Inspired by that same Spirit, Paul wrote to the churches in Galatia; James wrote to the believers scattered throughout the gentile world and, in the letter we call Revelation, John wrote to seven churches.

They are real churches and our first hermeneutical (interpretive) principle must always be: what did it mean to those original hearers? To determine that, we need to ask: "What was their setting?" And that is not a mystery either. Indeed, there are seven shorter, personalised messages within the long letter that tell us exactly what was happening in each of the churches. These give us a clue as to why this whole book was necessary.

Because of the persecution and resulting fears they may have felt, the victory of Christ is the theme, setting and foundational theology of this book. That is why it was such a blessing to them and why it has been a blessing to persecuted believers throughout history. From this wonderful book, we *know* that what happens in history happens because Jesus permits it as a part of his plan. It is a plan that cannot be overturned by his enemies; a plan established on the strength of a victory already won.

Key 5. Revelation often uses Old Testament images

Perhaps more than any other book, Revelation draws on Old Testament images and scenes. That is so important to know because it helps us with understanding its meaning. To describe the judgements of God, Revelation uses plagues just as when God brought Israel out of Egypt. It speaks of temples like Ezekiel does. In fact, at one stage John is styled like Ezekiel. We see him eating a scroll, as did Ezekiel, but yet he is different from Ezekiel in that he prophesies, not just about Israel, but about many nations and peoples and languages.

The witnesses of the Lamb are styled like Moses and Elijah.

Megiddo (Armageddon) is the geographical location of a great battle and one of the great songs of victory of the Old Testament, and it becomes the image of the defeat of all the enemies of Jesus, as he brings history to a close.

Why the use of such Old Testament images? The Holy Spirit continually draws on Old Testament images because these would have been familiar to the book's readers. They also give the *impression* that he wants to convey; they speak to the heart. The God who speaks through this book is one and the same as the God who wrought judgement and victory throughout the Old Testament, the God who is above and beyond all powers, all authorities and all nature.

This has always been the way of the prophets in Scripture. If you have a reasonable familiarity with the prophets, you will recognise that often they use the language of the Exodus to describe the deliverance that is coming through Christ. They use the language of their forefathers' slavery in Egypt to speak of bondage in Babylon. They style the coming Messiah like Moses. They speak of the coming King as a second appearing of David. The prophets speak of the new work of God (through the Messiah) as a new temple. But clearly Jesus was not a reincarnation of David, there was no second Egypt, and Jesus did not build a physical temple. Jesus was himself the new temple (John 2:19-22) and, as Peter and Paul describe, in him we are being built into the temple of God (1 Corinthians 3:16, 1 Peter 2:5). When God is speaking of the present and future, he uses language and events from Biblical history because the association of ideas helps us to understand the nature of what he is doing or promising. Revelation uses the same images for the same reason. To read them as literal recreations of the events of the Old Testament, really does not do justice to the way God speaks all through Scripture.

We do not attempt to make literal applications of every image in the Old Testament. Speaking through Jeremiah of the coming Babylonian captivity, God tells of a coming flood (Jeremiah 47:2); he tells of enemy horses that are going to eat Jerusalem (Jeremiah 8:16); and also of snakes that will bite and cannot be charmed (Jeremiah 8:17). Nowhere in Jeremiah's day or beyond did a flood come, horses eat Jerusalem, or snakes bite and kill. But we know how serious floods are when God sends them, as in Noah's day (Genesis 6). We know how serious snakes are when God sends them, as in Moses' day (Numbers 11). The message is not in the detail but in the power of the image. In Jeremiah's day, we don't look for three separate events: flood, horses and snakes. Each image speaks of the *same* event, the *same* human enemy, the *same* judgement. Revelation can be treated exactly the same way because it uses the same, or similar, Old Testament images to describe the work of God on earth, the victory of Christ and the judgement that will ultimately come.

You will find helicopters and Gorbachev and nuclear bombs in the book if you decide to read the images as secret messages and coded symbols for the initiated, but in doing so, you will rob the people of God of its timeless message. This book has been relevant *all through* history, not just since the advent of the Bell Helicopter Company or stealth bombers.

Key 6. Its relationship to and foundation upon the Gospel

This wonderful book we call Revelation only exists because of the Gospel! It takes its meaning and strength from the first coming of Christ. It is about the victory that was won at that time, the grace that ensues from that time, and the judgement that will come to those who reject God's redeeming King. It shows the drama behind the war against the saints by Satan and his kingdom, as he writhes under the consequences of his defeat on Golgotha. It shows the certainties that are ours despite the worst that Satan can do, because our future is secured in eternity by the one great act of obedience as the Lamb offered himself for us.

It was on the cross that Jesus won the victory. As Paul writes, God "disarmed the powers and authorities, he made a public spectacle of them, triumphing over them by the cross" (Colossians 2:15). No other action needs to take place in order to secure the victory. No authority in heaven or earth surpasses, undermines, weakens or intimidates that victory. Any teaching of the book of Revelation that leads believers to fearfully (or voyeuristically) concentrate on the enemy instead of the King of Kings and Lord of Lords is a very serious affront to the Gospel. Whole novels are written about people dealing with the antichrist, planning attacks against him, trying to outwit him. When were we ever given the liberty to deflect our attention from victor to vanquished? What a disgrace!

Throughout this book, we meet Jesus as Redeemer. We see ourselves in the light of his blood shed for us. We see him with his robe dipped in blood, and ourselves washed whiter than snow. It is in every sense a Gospel book.

Recently, I spoke with a young man from a Muslim nation, the son of the first believer from among his race of people. This young man came to Jesus at a young age, but said that, when he was a child, he was terrified of the second coming of Jesus. He was a believer, but had been so beset by the savage and sad projections about marks of beasts, plagues and every imaginable threat that he dreaded Jesus coming back. How sad, how terrible, that we should do this to children through popular books that seem to have a greater fascination with Satan than Christ. I had to admit that I was the same in my childhood and even as a young adult.

Oh, how frightened we were in my younger days as we waited for the European Common Market to reach its tenth member in fulfilment of the ten horns on the beast. Well, as with all speculations to date, those days are past. There has been no apology from the gurus who established their little prophetic empires by terrifying us. Time has moved on. Fools were made of the sincere people of God yet again, and perhaps the enemy laughs.

By God's grace, that young man now loves the thought of the return of Christ, unafraid because he is secure in Christ. So do I. As I said in the Introduction, I love this book of Revelation because I love the Gospel. Jesus' words to the twelve echo with resounding truth to all believers throughout all the centuries.

> "Fear not, little flock, for it is your Father's good pleasure to give you the kingdom."[4]

---

4   Luke 12:32 (RSV)

FOUR

A story told in opposites

Chapter 4

A story told in opposites

The images used to convey the truth throughout the book of Revelation are brilliant, not simply because they are universal and timeless, but because of the wonderful ways in which they work together. It is by understanding how the images work together that so much of the confusion is resolved.

Revelation is a book of opposites, and the message of the book takes its strength from the extremes of those opposites: height versus depth, light versus darkness, good versus evil. Once we see them, we realise that we just do not need to analyse them. They all but speak for themselves. Let's take a quick birds-eye view:

Right at the beginning we meet the Lamb of God. What becomes the opposite of a gentle, sacrificial Lamb? A dragon! And we see him in all his ugliness and fury as he wages his murderous warfare against the saints.

How does the dragon wage war against the saints? Through two beasts (chapter 13): the political kingdoms and religious systems of this world comprising the men and women who worship the dragon through these systems. Opposite these two earthly witnesses of the dragon are the two witnesses of the Lamb (chapter 11). The dragon has his witnesses, and God has his witnesses.

Those who belong to the kingdom of darkness are marked with the mark of the beast. The followers of the Lamb are marked with the mark of God and have his name written on them. They are opposites – God has marked his people, the kingdom of darkness has marked its people. One mark is the name of the Father and the Son, the other is the number of man. How much more do we need to know than that? How does it help to be trying to find tattoos that can somehow send people to hell?

The followers of the Lamb become the city of God, the New Jerusalem, the wife of the Lamb (21:9-10). The dragon will not be outdone – or so he thinks. He has his city, Babylon the great. But instead of it being a pure bride dressed in white linen, it is a prostitute, drunk with all of the evils of the earth. A bride and a prostitute – what could be a more graphic description of two opposing kingdoms?

The bride is invited to the great wedding feast of the Lamb. The people of the dragon also attend a feast, but they are on the menu (chapter 19)!

Out of the city of God and the throne flows a river of life as pure as crystal (chapter 22:1). Out of the mouth of the dragon flows a river of death and destruction (chapter 12:15).

What we see in all of this is not especially complicated. It is a message that is clear and profound. God has his people, and his Kingdom, established upon the work of the Lamb. Those people are sealed with his seal and will walk with him in white in his great city; indeed they are the city. God will wipe away all tears from their eyes and will be with them, and they with him, forever. Whatever God does Satan copies, but he can only create corruption. He is the opposite of everything that the Lamb is and creates only ugliness, corruption and death. The kingdom of this world, of which Satan said to Jesus, "I can give . . . to anyone I want to" (Luke 4:6b), ultimately goes with Satan into the lake of fire, tormented for ever and ever. The eternal city of God, indwelt by God and the Lamb, is magnificent in all of its unspeakable beauty. Babylon the great, Satan's city, is everything abhorrent and ugly. As a city, it is not anyone's bride but everyone's whore.

If we grasp nothing else but the nature of the opposites and the drama and power they convey, we will have grasped a major portion of the impact of the book. They tell us who is who and what is what, and they make us love the one and hate the other; long for the one and flee from the other.

FIVE

Revelation chapter 1

Chapter 5

Revelation chapter 1

Note: Throughout this book, I will not be including all of the passages in Revelation to which I am referring. It is strongly urged that you read the chapters of Revelation as they are referred to. Please don't presume you already know what they contain. Ignorance of what the text actually says has provided one of the greatest footholds for false and confusing teaching.

We have already observed that the *whole* book of Revelation is a letter addressed to specific groups of people (chapter 1:11). That is important to remember because, like any other letter of the New Testament, it would have been read out loud in the small, persecuted, back-room churches to which it was addressed.

John was in exile on Patmos and could not go to those churches. It appears that someone had come from each of the churches and would take the letter back with them. Those churches were not living in, or anywhere near, the last seven years of history (the time-frame some interpreters give to the whole book of Revelation). They were under the terrible storm clouds of persecution within the Roman Empire, and Jesus wanted them to have the message of this book to sustain them in the battle. So, there was a real day in real history when messengers from real churches came to John on Patmos and then returned with the letter under their arms. They stood in the meetings of their respective little fellowships and read this book.

As noted in the introduction, it is called a prophecy, but *not* like a Nostradamus "prophecy". It is not a collection of deep, coded mysteries to be unravelled by intuition and guesswork. It is a message to strengthen and encourage the beleaguered saints and to spur on those who were lagging behind. And surely, this first chapter has everything necessary for faithful hearts to burn with confidence and joy.

This first chapter answers the most fundamental questions underlying the whole book:

Who is Jesus?

He is the ruler of the kings of the earth – *now*, not in some future time. He is the firstborn from the dead, our pioneer. He is the very image of God, which is so deliberate and clear when we compare what we see of Jesus here and what we read of the Father in Daniel 7:9-14.

As I looked, thrones were set in place, and the Ancient of Days took his seat. His clothing was as white as snow; the hair of his head was white like wool. His throne was flaming with fire, and its wheels were all ablaze. A river of fire was flowing, coming out from before him. Thousands upon thousands attended him; ten thousand times ten thousand stood before him. The court was seated, and the books were opened . . . In my vision at night I looked, and there before me was one like a son of man, coming	I turned around to see the voice that was speaking to me. And when I turned I saw seven golden lampstands, and among the lampstands was someone "like a son of man", dressed in a robe reaching down to his feet and with a golden sash around his chest. His head and hair were white like wool, as white as snow, and his eyes were like blazing fire. His feet were like bronze glowing in a furnace, and his voice was like the sound of rushing waters.

with the clouds of heaven. He approached the Ancient of Days and was led into his presence.

He was given authority, glory and sovereign power; all peoples, nations and men of every language worshipped him. His dominion is an everlasting dominion that will not pass away, and his kingdom is one that will never be destroyed.

Daniel 7:9-14

In his right hand he held seven stars, and out of his mouth came a sharp double-edged sword. His face was like the sun shining in all its brilliance.

When I saw him, I fell at his feet as though dead. Then he placed his right hand on me and said: "Do not be afraid. I am the First and the Last.

I am the Living One; I was dead, and behold I am alive forever and ever! And I hold the keys of death and Hades."

Revelation 1:12-18

The phrases describing the appearance of the Father in Daniel 7 and the Son in Revelation 1 are almost identical. Not only that, but Jesus is the one who has the sharp two-edged sword, the fearful weapon of Roman justice in his mouth! Rome may well have made a kingdom for itself with its sharp two-edged swords strapped to the thighs of its legions of soldiers, but the Eternal One now being revealed has the sharp two-edged sword in his mouth. Just one blow from that one sword is enough to tear even Rome from its pedestal of arrogance.

He is "like a son of man". Daniel's great vision of the one like a son of man who receives all kingdoms, power and authority is fulfilled in none other than Jesus of Nazareth – obedient, crucified, risen and exalted. In Daniel's vision, the kingdom was given into the hands of the son of man, and now that son of man has come. He has died, risen, and lives forever more. He is the first and last, the one who alone holds the keys of death and the grave. Too much popular and fantasy literature (Christian or otherwise) speaks as if somehow Satan has the power of death and the ability to tear people prematurely from this world. They speak as if he rules a kingdom called hell as its despot. How utterly ridiculous! How belittling of Jesus! Jesus holds the keys, and the only time Satan will ever be in hell, he will be there as its prisoner; never, never, never as its ruler.

Who are we?

We are those who have been redeemed by the blood of this One, loved by him and set free by him. We have been made into a Kingdom of priests. Words once reserved for Old Testament Israel are now assigned to us, the new Israel.

What might we expect?

We can expect that, just as the Father kept the promise of the first coming of the King, so too will he keep the promise of the King's return for us. He will come, and when he comes there will be no mystery. Nothing will be hidden. Every eye will see him.

Who guarantees all of this?

The guarantee of his return for us comes from none other than the Alpha and Omega, the beginning and the end, the Lord God from eternity to eternity. In John's day, the Emperor Domitian demanded that the people call him "Lord God". What a joke! What folly of unimaginable proportions. It was megalomania to the point of utter insanity. God steps into John's world, cutting that little Roman tyrant down to size by announcing the absolute supremacy of Jesus. One day, even the Domitians of this world will weep and wail at the sight of the One coming in the clouds.

What a wonderful chapter for a suffering church. How their hearts must have burned within them when one day at one of their meetings, someone held up a parchment and said, "John has seen Jesus!" As the letter was read, they learned that Jesus *was* everything the prophets had described, and more.

Just one further note before we move on into chapter 2. The Holy Spirit is referred to as the seven spirits; or seven-fold Spirit. Why? It is probably as simple as the fact that there are seven churches, and that the Spirit is given to every church. Later, Jesus is described as having seven eyes, perhaps to indicate that he sees every one of those churches. Jesus sees each of them, and the Spirit is given to each of them. If you don't try and make Jesus have seven literal eyes, then don't worry too much about trying to make God have seven Holy Spirits! Sometimes with explanations, I think simple is best.

SIX

"I know your deeds . . ."
Revelation chapters 2 and 3

Chapter 6

"I know your deeds . . ."
Revelation chapters 2 and 3

In chapter 1, we are shown a symbol, the meaning of which is explained to us. We see Jesus as the One who stands among the lampstands and it is explained to us that the lampstands are the seven churches to which the letter is written. In chapters 2 and 3, we have an individual message to each of those churches, a letter within a letter. The natural question is: how do they fit? What is the function of these individually addressed letters within the overall letter?

It may well be that someone in the churches to whom this whole letter of Revelation was written would say to Jesus, "If only you knew. If only you could really understand what is happening here in our situation." The truth is that Jesus *did* know what was happening in their churches! He *did* know their circumstances. Jesus is not just in glory, not just risen, exalted and remote, but he is among the churches. He is so close, so much a part of them that he can say, "I know your deeds." In fact, he can even say, "I know you have a reputation, but I know the reality behind the reputation."

These letters remove the distance the churches might feel from a Jesus who is now in glory. Far from being a distraction from the main message, these letters bring the main message of the book home to the individual churches far more strongly because the one speaking to them knows them intimately. He knows them because he sees beyond the obvious; below the surface.

Much has been written about these seven letters. There are some very good and helpful expositions based upon them, and some very helpful historical information that can make the message even more focused. Therefore, we will just spend a very brief time on them, looking at the main issues involved in each one, leaving the more detailed analyses to others.

As we look at the letters, we will easily see that Jesus usually describes himself in a way that becomes applicable to the current situation of each church. He has a word of commendation and a word of criticism for each. He also makes a promise to each church.[5] As we look at them, we need to be careful to treat them as we would any other New Testament letter. In Colossians, Philippians and Thessalonians, for example, things are said that relate to the readers' specific situations. However, we do not treat the warnings and promises in those letters as unique to those churches. We see them as having an ongoing application to all believers at all times. We begin where they were, we understand what is written as they understood it, and then having understood what was said to them, we apply the message to ourselves today. So too with these seven letters.

For example, "To him who overcomes, I will give the right to eat from the tree of life, which is in the paradise of God" (written to Ephesus, 2:7). Must we suppose that the only believers in all of the history of the church who will eat of the tree of life in the paradise of God will be those who were born in Ephesus in the first century? Of course not! Each of the promises, warnings and encouragements applies to us all, but perhaps speaks to our hearts

---

5   A good way to study these letters is to draw up a chart with the following column headings: Description of Jesus; Word of commendation; Word of complaint; Warning; Promise.

to a greater or lesser degree according to the character and conduct of our own church's life at the time we read it. Again, it is the same as other letters in the New Testament. If, as a church, you are beginning to feel the tensions of strained relationships, then the letter to the Philippians is especially relevant to you at this time. If you are battling false teachers, perhaps the letter to the Colossians is especially relevant. This will also be the case with each of these letters to the seven churches.

The Angel of the churches?

You will note that each letter is written "To the angel of the church in..." The Greek word for "angel" is the simple word "messenger". It is the context that determines whether it is referring to a heavenly messenger or a human one. In this instance, simple is best. It is unlikely that Jesus would actually have John write a letter to an angel! (How would it be delivered?) John was on Patmos, unable to leave. How would his letter get to the seven churches? Someone would come from each church and take it back home with them; perhaps someone in leadership. So while the whole book, which is one complete letter, is for all the churches, these letters are *specifically* "to the messenger from the church in . . ." Simple is best!

Let's now wander through the letters.

Ephesus – Chapter 2:1-7

What was the key issue? Ephesus was a church that had done so much. Not only that, but it was doctrinally sound. It would not put up with false teachers, but could recognise them. It had endured hardships for the sake of Christ. However, there was a problem they had not recognised – their love had begun to grow cold. Love for each other or love for God? It is the same thing. If we do not love each other, we cannot say we love God. (John's first letter, the one we call 1 John, speaks long and loud about that subject!)

Is it possible for a modern church to be powering along, intolerant of false teachers, standing passionately on their five points of this or four points of that, making sure everyone toes the line doctrinally, even pushing ahead against the winds of hardship, and yet not showing love to each other? Is it possible that continually seeking out theological error can lead those with minimal knowledge to feel insecure and unloved? Yes, it is. Sound doctrine is extremely important, but not if it is used as a weapon against those who may not yet have come to the same understanding. Truth is not a replacement for love.

The warning is serious: "I will remove the lampstand from its place" (verse 5). Have you ever known big, doctrinally passionate churches to stand forlorn on street corners, the "light" having moved elsewhere? Do you think it is possible that the life, energy, true witness and presence of Christ have been removed, making them as attractive as a blackout? The Spirit and power of Jesus is not among them any more, but has moved on to another place? Yes indeed, and some cities are littered with such monuments to coldness.

The remedy is covered by three verbs – remember, repent and do. The third is of most significance. It is not about rekindling emotions; it is about *doing* what we did at first. It is a call to action. In the beginning, did we love to visit each other, pray with each other, give to each other, eat with each other, and weep with each other? In the beginning, did we put up with each other's doctrinal and spiritual weaknesses as we loved each other through the growth pains? Then do those things again, irrespective of feelings.

The Ephesian church is promised that they will eat from the tree of life in the paradise of God. Eating was the central point of church life in the first century; their love-feasts, where Jews and Gentiles, slave and free, male and female all ate together, demonstrating the reality of the death of Christ. Love and "family" were demonstrated at the meal table.[6] Perhaps that is why the promise to this church is framed in this way. Perhaps Jesus is saying, "Eat with each other now, in love, as you did at the beginning, because you will one day eat together in my home."

When we believed in Christ, we were ushered into a new family. Families are about relationships. Let's take the warning.[7]

Smyrna – Chapter 2:8-11

Smyrna was a very beautiful and important city, but Smyrna had two characteristics that made it a constant danger for believers. The major presenting danger was that it was a centre for Caesar-worship.

Rome was a vast empire with many different races, cultures and religions. It was felt by the central authorities in Rome that one religious concept was needed to unify the people, while continuing to allow them to exercise their own private religions. The one person who embodied the whole concept of the great Roman Empire was Caesar – in him the spirit of Rome assumed a visible form. So it became official policy that the emperor was a god. To refuse to worship the emperor in addition to your other

---

6   Consider the serious consequences in Corinth, a church whose eating together had divided between rich and poor, the haves and the have-nots (1 Corinthians 11). See THE GATHERING, Ray Barnett, Littleman Publishing, 2010, for a fuller treatment of the issues of church relationships and eating together at the Lord's Supper.

7   Who are the Nicolaitans? Sadly, there is not enough historical information to accurately determine who they were. There are theories, of course. Perhaps they were the group who first began to divide the people of God between clergy and laity. That is not a bad theory, growing out of the nature of the name by which the group was called. However we cannot be sure. So stick with what you do know, not with what you do not know. The letter to Ephesus says enough to us even if we cannot know accurately who the Nicolaitans were.

gods was not just a religious issue, it was regarded as an act of treason, and in Rome *that* was serious!

The second problem was the Jewish population. The Roman empire had granted the Jewish population exemption from the need to offer incense to Caesar, and in the early stages, because Rome regarded the followers of Jesus as a sect of Judaism, the Christians were also exempted. However, as jealousies and tensions increased between the Jews and the people of Jesus, the Jewish population became informers against the Christians, declaring them to be an independent, non-Jewish religion. This meant that the believers were no longer covered by the Jewish exemption. They were therefore committing treason by not worshipping the emperor. The Jewish leaders incited the governors to persecute believers, and also persecuted the believers themselves. It was the Jewish leaders who instigated the famous martyrdom of Polycarp. On a feast day they grabbed him, dragged him to the market place and demanded that he worship Caesar or die. His famous answer was, "Sixty-eight years I have served Christ, and he has never done me wrong. How can I blaspheme my King who saved me?" And he was beaten and burned to death right then and there.

As William Barclay puts it, "In Smyrna, the church was a place for heroes."[8] Many believers throughout the centuries have been under such pressure; many have shared in the afflictions of Smyrna. Let's look at what Jesus says to these dear saints.

Jesus introduces himself as the one who died and was made alive. In this one statement, Jesus identifies that he has walked the pathway of rejection and death before them. What is more, he himself is the absolute proof that though they die, yet they also will live.[9] As their faithful high priest, Jesus knows exactly what they face, the fears and the pain. He has stood where they now stand,

---

8   Barclay, Letters to the Seven Churches, SCM London, 1964 p35

9   In John 11:25-26, Jesus said to Martha, "I am the resurrection and the life. He who believes in me will live, even though he dies; and whoever lives and believes in me will never die. Do you believe this?"

but one day they will stand where he now is, alive forever more. Jesus knows the real situation of their church, and also knows who their enemies are. Jesus describes them as "a synagogue of Satan". By this phrase, he openly identifies them as children of Abraham in name but not by conviction. They call themselves Jews but are not doing God's work. They are doing the work of the enemy. They are slanderers and destroyers of God's people for economic or political gain.

For Smyrna, the days of persecution will be brief, ("ten days" is a way of saying "just a short while") but it will also be intense. They will suffer imprisonment and even death for the sake of Jesus. Because they refused to worship Caesar, everything might be taken from them – worldly possessions, even life itself. But Jesus knows they are truly rich.

To these beleaguered people, Jesus affirms the great and wondrous reality of the Gospel, something which he alone could achieve for them by his own life, suffering and death. For these saints, these martyrs, there will be "the crown of life".

Don't imagine the people of Smyrna as a select group walking around heaven wearing special hats with the word "Life" written on it! The crowns they receive, their reward, will *itself* be *life*.[10] Nor will the saints of Smyrna be the only ones in history to receive Life – all who believe in Jesus receive eternal life as their crown and reward.

---

10 Check the following ways in which Scripture speaks of "crowns". "Blessings crown the head of the righteous, but violence overwhelms the mouth of the wicked" (Proverbs 10:6). "A wife of noble character is her husband's crown, but a disgraceful wife is like decay in his bones" (Proverbs 12:4). "The wealth of the wise is their crown, but the folly of fools yields folly" (Proverbs 14:24). "Grey hair is a crown of splendour; it is attained by a righteous life" (Proverbs 16:31). "Children's children are a crown to the aged, and parents are the pride of their children" (Proverbs 17:6). To imagine the word crown as meaning something worn literally on the head would have a wealthy man with his wife, his children and bags of money sitting on his head! He doesn't wear those things as a crown; those things *are* his crown. For believers, life eternal will be our crown, our reward.

But here, the promise is directed at a point of need. Jesus so beautifully reminds these troubled people of their eternity. Hold on! I died and am alive forever more; you may die for my sake, but you too will live.

All of the promises in these letters are universal for all believers, but they are things of which specific groups need to be reminded in their specific situations. If I say to a weeping person, "One day, God will dry your tears and you will see Jesus as he is", I am not suggesting that that person is the only one in Christian history for whom this will happen. I am comforting *that* person with *those specific* words of certainty in their *specific* time of need. As a further illustration, to the people beside the lake, Jesus was the bread of life. To the woman at the well, he was living water. To the blind man, he was a good shepherd. These are not promises exclusively for those people. Jesus is all of those to all his people.

For those who overcome, there is escape from the second death, something that all their enemies will face.

The overcomers?

At this point, we need to think about the commonly used term "those who overcome". Who are they? If they are a select group of believers, then the promises of life, paradise, reigning with Christ and so on, are only for a select group of believers. We *know* that cannot be true because it is contrary to the Gospel! The Gospel must always be the lens through which we look at Scripture. It is the Gospel that keeps our interpretations on track.

The Gospel declares that all who have believed in Jesus will reign with Christ in paradise. We will all inherit eternal life. Otherwise, the work of Christ for us is incomplete and our faith in him is not enough. So we cannot make this term divide believers into two groups. It would be contrary to what we know to be true of the Gospel. So then, who are the overcomers? This whole book we call Revelation is the greatest description of the victory of Christ in Scripture. Here we meet Jesus, in all his glory, as the One who has overcome sin, the grave and the world. And we are in him.[11] Therefore, in him, we too are overcomers. It is not a word used as a threat – "Overcome or perish!" It is a word used as an encouragement for the saints. Remember that this book was written to strengthen believers for the battle, not to pull the rug out from under their confidence in Christ! The message of Jesus, to his suffering saints in Smyrna and throughout the ages, is that each of us in Christ, as his overcomers, will receive the promises he has made. His promises are certain, including the promise to keep us to the end. In other words, to make us overcome.[12]

The overcomers *will* escape the second death. This is a message of hope! The promises are expressed in terms that met the needs of the church at the time: Do not be afraid. Love for Christ on earth may bring death, but it brings life in eternity. Like Christ, we die to live. Conversely, rejection of Christ may save a man's life on earth, but in the end it will bring something far worse – the second death. As Jesus warned us, "For whoever wants to save their life will lose it, but whoever loses their life for me will save it." (Luke 9:24)

Pergamum – Chapter 2:12-17

Pergamum was probably the greatest city in Asia Minor. By the time John wrote, it had been a capital city for over 300 years. It

---

11   "In Christ" is a constant theme of our New Testament. We have been placed into him so that his experience becomes our experience, his life becomes our life, his victory becomes our victory and his glory becomes our glory. He reigns and we reign. He lives and we live. He triumphed over all his enemies and so do we as we enter into the eternal city. The worst our enemies can do is cause physical death, but death cannot hold us. In Christ, we have overcome the world.

12   If you have any personal concerns about this, let Jesus speak to you. Read his words in John 6:35-40 and John 10:27-30. There are many other passages of course, but read what Jesus said and let him speak to you.

had formerly been part of the empire of Alexander the Great but chose to become part of the Roman Empire voluntarily. So it was not Roman by conquest but by choice. Like Smyrna, it was a centre of Caesar worship, and perhaps the most significant of all such centres in the region. Indeed, for forty years it had been a centre of imperial worship. Was that why it was called "Satan's seat"? Perhaps. Another reason could be that official persecution of believers in the Roman Empire began in Pergamum.

There was also in the city a major temple and altar to "Zeus the Saviour". People would come to the temple from all over the world to be healed of diseases. They would spend a night in the temple in the dark, along with tame and harmless snakes. As they lay there in the dark, if a snake touched them it was regarded as the touch of god himself. In fact, they worshipped snakes as animal gods.

Remarkable for us is that, in the midst of the city that was the most devoted worshipper of Caesar and had the altar to "Zeus the Saviour", there were Christians – our brothers and sisters – who had not denied Christ. They were in danger 365 days a year, but they had stood firm.

Antipas is singled out as a faithful witness, or martyr. While there is limited concrete historical information, legend says that he was roasted alive in a brass bull. He was a faithful witness unto death. Were that legend to be true, its effect on the other believers would have been sobering in the extreme! The cities of the day were not huge like our modern cities. They would have been much smaller, rather like large towns to us. Having a brother perish in such a way in the midst of your town would shake you to the core. Would you be next? But still these brethren stayed true to the faith.

To the believers in this centre of imperial worship, Jesus speaks as the One who holds the sharp two-edged sword. In Roman society, at government level, the two-edged sword was the sign of authority and justice. It indicated just who held the power over life and death! To the people of Pergamum, the message is clear – their times and seasons are in the hands of Jesus, *not* the hands of the local authorities nor Caesar in Rome. However the believers in Pergamum faced dangers other than just the Roman authorities.

There was a time during Israel's exodus when they came against the Moabites. The king of Moab determined to defeat or destroy Israel and so urged Balaam the prophet to come and curse them.[13] But he could not. God would not allow Balaam's mouth to be filled with curses against his people. And so Israel withstood an external threat. But that is not where the story ends. Later, in chapter 31 of Numbers, we discover that Balaam advised some of the women of idolatrous Moab to enter the camp of the Israelites and seduce them. This they did, and even intermarried with Israelites. And so God's people, strong against *external* attack, began to crumble on the *inside* through an attack far more subtle and appealing.

Could it happen again? Jesus says yes, and points Pergamum to the danger they face in this regard. Eating meat offered to idols was not a problem, as we are clearly taught in Corinthians[14], but participating in idol feasts was. Idol feasts became orgies, orgies became idol worship and step-by-step, immorality began to invade this embattled little church. These dear people had stood firm against persecution, but now they were in danger of being defeated by immorality and idolatry, just as Israel had been. This would mean the church would cease to be an effective force. It would become just a variation of Roman culture under a different religious name.

Let's take the caution! *Satan not only persecutes, he seduces.* Here we have a church in which Satan can work by exerting pressures

---

13   You can read of these events in Numbers chapters 22 to 24.
14   See 1 Corinthians chapters 8, 9 10.

from a pagan, immoral society. The attack from outside, the direct hard attack, did not succeed. However, the strategy of offering what the sinful human heart desires does succeed. Sadly, today there are so many preachers, like Balaam, offering exactly what everyone in the kingdom of this world wants – wealth, health and power. How wonderful, how seductive, to be offered a faith in which all sense of suffering is gone and in which we can drive the streets of our towns in the best of cars, wearing designer clothes and in perfect health. They tell us that we can achieve all our personal and career goals, and take our places at society's top end.

How easy it would be to take up our crosses and follow Christ if that cross could simply be hung in the window of a luxury car or worn as a fashion accessory over designer clothes.

Yes, Satan not only attacks, he seduces. And he renders churches ineffective. The issue is not wealth per se, but making wealth and prosperity a perk of the Gospel.

Imagine a huge church, thousands of people, every one with a passionate desire to become rich like the world around them; to have a life of ease and health. Their desire is to attract the world to a Jesus whose suffering brought us health, wealth and happiness in a life of ease. It would be attractive because most people want a dose of religion – but without sacrifice. Such a church could easily attract numbers, huge numbers in fact. But how effective do you think such a church might really be in tearing down the strongholds of the enemy? The strongholds of the enemy and the seat of idolatry are not in movie theatres and bars, they are in the mind. Minds anchored to the thought processes of a culture that creates happiness without God. It is all too easy to sanctify the material goals of this world and make them into "Christian" goals, or rewards. Yes, Satan not only persecutes, he seduces.

In our age, are we seeing a move towards becoming just a religious version of our secular culture – big, successful, socially powerful – but not looking much like the Carpenter of Nazareth at all? It is serious food for thought. "Dear children, keep yourselves from idols," wrote John (1 John 5:21).

And the promise? Those who refuse to eat the bread of idols on this earth will have the bread of God, manna – food reserved for God's people alone – in the New Jerusalem. And the white stone? Probably the best explanation I have come across is that in Rome a successful gladiator, at the end of his career, would be given a white stone as a sign of his successful retirement. That stone meant his career was over; he was free. He never had to fight again. If ever he was challenged, or his old masters wanted to make money from him again, he could show them his white stone. He could rest, and no one could call him a coward.

To the saints in Pergamum, Jesus promises just such a stone. Yes, my brothers and sisters, the day *will* come when the battles will be over, forever!

Thyatira – Chapter 2:18-29

Jezebel is an infamous name from the Old Testament, a name almost synonymous with certain kinds of evil. Jezebel came from outside Israel, married King Ahab, and although an outsider, she exercised such an influence in the kingdom that eventually it seemed all Israel had gone over to the worship of Baal. Jesus introduces the name Jezebel in his comments about the church in Thyatira.

Thyatira was a great church! Jesus' words about it in 2:19 are wonderful, "I know your deeds, your love and faith, your service and perseverance, and that you are now doing more than you did at first." What a tremendous commendation. Most of us would want our church described in such a way. However, this church was also in serious danger.

It may have been one particular person, it may even have been a prophetess actually called Jezebel, but that is neither necessary nor likely. Balaam was not in Pergamum, and it need not be necessary for a real Jezebel to be in Thyatira. Whoever it was, or whatever group is being spoken about, they were having Jezebel's effect – seducing the people to follow the idols of their time (1 Kings 16:29ff). Left unchecked, just as in Ahab's Israel, the true worship of God in Thyatira would be submerged under the reigning idolatry of the day.

But is it really possible for good, faithful people to be led astray in such serious ways? Yes indeed! Idols do not necessarily need to be ugly little figurines set on pedestals. Idols are those things to which we turn for fulfilment, or meaning in life, apart from God himself. As mentioned in the previous section, the offers of wealth and power can become idolatrous pursuits leading to spiritual and literal immorality. In recent times, we have seen elevated Christian leaders, obsessed with wealth and power, rush headlong down a pathway to immorality. How the church has been shamed in these last decades by men and women who were offered all the kingdoms of this world through the lens of a TV camera, plunging into debauchery and utterly crass materialism. If it can happen to those in the public eye, might it not also happen to their followers? Is there also a possibility that cultic, even occultic leaders can come into the church from outside and teach error in glittering, glamorous and attractive ways, leading the people to find their satisfaction in the offerings of this world? Indeed!

One modern popular TV preacher, hero-worshipped by millions, openly admits to reviving his spiritual power by lying on the graves of two dead prophetesses. Another, famed for offering believers all the material prosperity they might want, openly teaches that Jesus was defeated by Satan on the cross. He also teaches that God, "the greatest failure in the Bible"[15], lives

---

15   Copeland, Kenneth 1988, Praise-a-Thon, TBN, April, cited in Hanegraaff, H 1993, Christianity in Crisis, Harvest House Publishers, Oregon

on a planet like ours, stands a little over six feet tall, and weighs around 250 pounds.

These things are not Biblical Christianity in any shape or form. So why do such preachers become so popular? Because they offer what unbelieving Israel wanted – signs and wonders. Jesus called sign-seeking Israel a "wicked and adulterous generation".[16]

They also offer the most seductive of what the kingdom of this world has on offer – the opportunity to be like the nations around them, with the shame and stumbling block of the cross submerged under a truckload of wealth and power. Perhaps Jezebel *can* still find her way among us more easily than we might imagine. And she can produce illegitimate children today, just as she did in Thyatira's day.

The warning from Jesus is that he will take action. Three groups or types of people are then mentioned as being on the receiving end of those actions. The first group or person, Jezebel, will be cast onto a bed of suffering. Her time for repentance has passed.

The second group, her children, those born of Jezebel and who are not really the people of God, will be struck dead. They have no place or inheritance among the Lord's people.

And the third group, those who have come under her influence and committed adultery with her, will be cast onto a bed of suffering unless (and until) they repent. For the Lord's people, foolish and led astray, there is still opportunity to repent. Jesus knows those who are his. He also assesses a person's works, and will reward accordingly.

For the faithful in Thyatira, there is a gentle and gracious message from Jesus. He lays no greater burden on them, but asks

---

16 "Then some of the Pharisees and teachers of the law said to him, 'Teacher, we want to see a miraculous sign from you.' He answered, 'A wicked and adulterous generation asks for a miraculous sign! But none will be given it except the sign of the prophet Jonah'" (Matthew 12:38-39). Please note that this did not stop Jesus from performing miracles. And he can still perform miracles today. The issue here was unbelief and the quest for just one more miracle to satisfy the double-minded.

them only to hold onto what they have. Perhaps in Thyatira they will never have the social power and connections that come from worshipping the idols of their local trade guild. Perhaps they may even lose their jobs or businesses because of their refusal to follow Jezebel. But one day they will rule the nations with Jesus. He will give them the morning star – perhaps a local cultural symbol, or perhaps it speaks of Jesus himself (Chapter 22:16). And for you today, perhaps you won't have the wealth that the TV charlatans say is your right as a believer. Perhaps you will never seem to have the power that they have. But know this: one day you will rule the nations. Don't clamour after what you don't have, but hold firmly on to what you do have.

Sardis – Chapter 3:1-6

What things give a church a reputation for being alive? In most cultures it is big numbers, big budgets, big buildings, great music with high power "worship leaders" and even doctrinally sound teaching. Those are the things people see and hear. But they are not the only things that Jesus sees. Here he looks at a church with a name for being alive – whatever that might have meant in the first century – and knows the reality. They are dead and asleep – both conditions are said to apply. Such is the condition of Sardis.

Five things combine to form the remedy Jesus sets out for Sardis:

1. *Awaken* – Shake yourselves spiritually. Snap out of your lethargy.

2. *Strengthen* what remains – Look at those things that are good and true in your church and strengthen them. Don't let those things crumble and die.

3. *Remember* – In fact the original language suggests *keep on remembering continuously* what you have been given and what you

have heard. Remember the Gospel. Remember all that Christ has done for you and the implications for your life.

4. *Obey* it – Keep on obeying it.

5. *Repent* – Turn around from your old ways; a change of mind and direction. In other words, make the decision and stick to it.

Jesus warns them that he will come like a thief. At a time when they are least expecting it, Jesus will step into the life of this church and deal with it. It will be a surprise visit; thieves are never expected!

I was impressed by reading of the time when Alexander the Great reached Sardis and could not conquer it. Behind Sardis was a citadel, or fortress, high up on a rock platform that presented as a sheer cliff, apparently impossible to scale. Obsessed with conquest, Alexander offered a great reward to any soldier who could find a way up that cliff. One day, one of his soldiers saw a man from the citadel drop his helmet down into the valley. Alexander's soldier watched as the man from Sardis climbed down the cliff, picked up his helmet and scaled back up. He watched intently, etching the track into his memory. He then assembled a small band of hand-picked soldiers and retraced the steps of that man from Sardis up the cliff. When they reached the fortress, they found it completely unguarded, presumably because the garrison on duty simply could not believe that anyone could possibly find their way up the cliff like that. They were supposed to be on guard, but were asleep. That is the history of Sardis and the danger of this church. They have a name for being alive but are dead. They are asleep. They are not on guard.

But some in the church in Sardis have remained faithful, and Jesus makes two wonderful promises to them. They will walk with Christ in white robes and they will never be blotted out of the book of life. Those are promises that also hold true for all believers. However, here they are presented afresh to Sardis so that its people might have the courage to hold on, and the motivation to strengthen what remains in their church. It may be hard, but it will be worth it.

In every city there was a register of citizens, those living in the city. As they died they were removed from that book. Not so with those who belong to Jesus! Those who belong to Jesus will never be blotted out because you never die! You are secure, you will live, so press on against the tide.

Philadelphia – Chapter 3:7-13

The more common view of this letter is that it relates to mission endeavour, a view usually held by those who see these letters as a portrait of church history. Within that portrait, this church is seen as being the true church. Jesus had set before them an open door for mission, and *this* door, no one could shut. However, I wonder if that is really what Jesus is pointing to.

A greater problem for the churches suffering within the Roman Empire was the possibility of a sense of insecurity. The message of Christ was spreading, just as it is today in nations closed to the Gospel and where believers are persecuted for their faith. You can imagine the types of emotional and spiritual stresses that could come when churches, so soon after the resurrection of Christ, were being engulfed by a world in which Jesus appeared to lack control. Serious questions would have arisen. Did the persecution indicate a return to the days of Babylon? Had they been tried and found wanting, only to be cast out of the Kingdom, just as Israel was put out of the land? Was Jesus in control, or the Roman army? Were they really secure in Christ and was his Kingdom truly an unshakeable, everlasting Kingdom?

The Philadelphians are being ground down by the "synagogue of Satan", as were those in Smyrna. They had little strength, but had kept the Word of Jesus. They were faithful despite their weakness in the face of persecution. At this season, do they need to hear about an open door for mission? Or do they need to hear that the door into his Kingdom, and eventually into eternal glory, is one that Jesus has opened for them and one that only Jesus can shut? His is the authority over their destiny. The door to eternal rest is not one that Rome or anyone else can shut.

These beleaguered saints were to be given the keys of David. They could enter the presence of the king, and no one could shut them out. Additionally, they would become a pillar in the temple of God. No one will be able to take away their crown, and they will never have to leave that Kingdom. Their enemies, the "synagogue of Satan", will ultimately fall at their feet.

This is important to us today, and especially for our brothers and sisters in oppressed and persecuted lands. It is something we have seen enacted throughout history. Totalitarian governments have *not* been able to prevent people coming to Christ or staying in Christ. In fact the harder they work at preventing it, the more people seem to press towards the open door. The more difficult their lives become, the more they cling to the promise that nothing shall ever pluck them from the hand of the Father. Jesus did not become King of Kings and Lord of Lords only to surrender the eternal destiny of his people to some petty bureaucrat or mini tyrant whose reign is little more than a punctuation mark on the pages of history. Yes, localised authority seems to be strong, but the door to the Kingdom is opened or shut by Jesus alone! For those of us who have believed, the door has been opened, never to close again.

The believers in Philadelphia are commended by Jesus because, in the face of the difficulties presented by life in the Roman Empire, they have remained true to the Word of God. They have endured with patience and been faithful. What a tremendous encouragement to them and to believers all throughout history who have lived in seasons of repression. It may be that some believers today look at lands where freedom reigns and feel themselves to be so weak and ineffective. They may wonder if the King is pleased. What a joy to know that the King *is* pleased. He looks at their perseverance and their faithfulness with deep, eternal love and *is* pleased.

The Philadelphians would be kept from the hour of trial. This is not an easy statement. Does Jesus mean a trial soon to come, in the first century, or is he speaking of the final judgement? Perhaps it is both localised and forward-looking. More than likely the emphasis here is on the end of all things and the judgements that would come upon the earth. But also note that this promise is not only for the Philadelphians. Are the believers in Philadelphia the only ones in history to escape the final judgement, that "hour of trial"? No. It is a guarantee inherent in the Gospel that anyone who has believed in Jesus "will not come under judgement but has passed from death to life".[17]

In Philadelphia, one of the ways that the city's leading citizens were honoured, was to have their name written on a pillar in the temple. For the believers in Philadelphia, so abused and dishonoured by their culture, there was a far greater honour awaiting. They would have the name of God, the name of the city of Jerusalem, and the name of Jesus written on them. And even beyond that, the believers will *themselves* stand as pillars in the temple. Long after all the pillars of all the temples of all the cities of earth have been ground to powder by the ravages of time and judgements of eternity, these saints will stand as pillars in the temple, trophies of the grace of God throughout all the ages of eternity. And they will never have to leave again. As King David wrote, "I will dwell in the house of the LORD forever".[18]

---

17   John 5:24 (NRSV)
18   Psalm 23:6

Laodicea – Chapter 3:14-22

Laodicea is the most well known of the names of the seven churches, probably because we are more fascinated by complaints and criticisms than commendations. Just about everyone can tell you about the "wretched, pitiable, poor, blind and naked" Laodicea, while being rather less certain about the subject matter of each of the other letters. And yet the criticisms of the church and message of the letter are no less real, despite their almost folklore notoriety.

Laodicea was a wealthy church in a wealthy town. Wealth has ruined more people than poverty, or as Winston Churchill once said, "Success has ruined more men than failure." And in the Kingdom of God, that is also true. The easiest and most certain way of destroying the impact of the Gospel is to align it with money or prosperity. Whenever we crave an abundance of the things that can anchor us into the kingdom of this world, we are in danger of spiritual decline. Decline *need* not happen, as men like Abraham and Job have shown us. They saw their wealth for what it was, and its source was always acknowledged. But the human heart is fickle and is easily drawn away.

Generalisations are not often helpful, but it is interesting to reflect on the focus and priority of churches in wealthy Western countries as compared to their persecuted, poverty-stricken brothers and sisters under oppressive regimes. As I travel, I meet people from both sides of the poverty-persecution divide. When asked about their churches, Western believers usually speak of the blessing of God in terms of their new buildings, their numbers and the quality of their "worship music". Often money is mentioned. Among persecuted people, where I spend so much of my time, the response is usually very, very different, with material accoutrements almost never part of the discussion.

The Laodicean church basked in the prosperity of its culture, and Jesus speaks to them in exactly those terms. Laodicea's industries were varied and renowned. One was its clothing manufacture. A special breed of sheep in the region produced highly prized wool which was exported all over the world, bringing great wealth to the town. But Jesus says of the church, "You are naked!" Laodicea was also famous for an eye ointment for weak and sickly eyes. It was exported all over the world in tablet form and then ground down and applied quite effectively to the eyes. Jesus tells these people that they are blind and urges them to buy ointment for their eyes.

There were mineral springs outside of the city that were lukewarm. In one of the countries in which I spend some time, there is a plethora of mineral springs, and while they may have some sort of beneficial effect for bathers (even if it is mind over matter!), the smell of the water is such that it almost makes me sick just to have it waft past my nose! I can't imagine what would happen if I drank it. It seems that Laodicea's springs were just like that. Despite its therapeutic reputation, the lukewarm water of the springs was such that, if you drank it, it made you sick. Jesus speaks of the church as lukewarm and that he would spew it out of his mouth. (Don't press the images too far, they are just images. The church is not in Jesus' mouth and Jesus doesn't vomit! It is just a dramatic illustration.)

What was actually wrong with the church? They were at ease, and the fire had gone out of their walk with Christ. It may have had many manifestations, but the heat of their commitment was gone. They were walking in such a comfortable compromise with the affluent culture of their day that they called forth the very strongest of words from Christ. They were wealthy, secure and felt the need of nothing, presumably not even Christ! (Why should we pray "Give us this day our daily bread" when we have abundant wealth?) In reality, they were spiritually poor, blind, and naked. They had become a religious version of their secular culture and prized the things that anchored them to the kingdom of this world.

The church will never regain its prophetic voice while it mimics Babylon in its desires and measures of success.

Most alarmingly, Jesus is actually outside the church trying to get back in. Presumably the programmes, the administration and the functions are all rolling along nicely and no one even notices that Jesus is not there. No one even hears him knocking. However, for the ones in the church who do hear him knock, and who want a renewed and revitalised fellowship with Christ, the promise is always there. Open to him, and he *will* come in and *will* eat with you and *will* have fellowship. That is always the deepest desire of Jesus, to have true fellowship with his people.[19]

Letters for all believers through all of history

Our walk through the seven letters has not been exhaustive. We have simply seen enough to know that these letters have a first century meaning and also a timeless message. By measuring our experiences against theirs, we can take from these letters what Jesus would say to us, just as we do from every other letter in the New Testament. All of the pressures upon these first century churches are potentially awaiting us in our generation. As the seasons of political and cultural life ebb and flow throughout history and around the world, we will find the same types of temptations and internal and external attacks coming against us. Through it all, Christ is watching over us and is in our midst. That is a great comfort but also brings a sobering caution. He sees, he knows and he measures our actions as local churches.

It is worth asking the question at this stage whether the text of these letters has given any indication that they represent the seven ages of church history? It is a theory that has gained considerable

---

19 As you can see, chapter 3:20 is not about personal evangelism and never has been. That came as the result of a lovely but theologically dubious painting. The statement is written to churches, and by making it an evangelistic verse, we miss what Jesus is saying to us, especially if we live in freedom and affluence.

currency in some places. According to that theory, we can look at each letter and see it as a description of one of the successive ages and seasons of the history of the church.

That theory, like so many others related to Revelation, has been created outside the Scriptures and been forced into the Scriptures.

Apart from it being a figment of someone's imagination, in its sweeping generalisations, the seven-ages theory is a terrible affront to Christ and his church. The advocates of this theory tell us that we are in the Laodicean era. The letter to Laodicea may well be a serious warning to us if we live in a wealthy Western country, but in this early twenty-first century, would you call the church in Sudan Laodicean? Or the house-churches in China? What about the believers in North Korea, or Iran, or Saudi Arabia? What about the churches suffering under Hindu fanaticism in India, or political thuggery in regimes across Africa, Asia and especially Central Asia? What a disgrace to make pronouncements about God's people being in a generalised Laodicean era! How dare we view the world as if it revolves around our Western experience. The West is not the centre of the world, nor are we the bench mark of anything! We have brothers and sisters in "Smyrna" right now, persecuted, imprisoned, being skinned alive, burned alive, and crucified. Will we go to them and lament their Laodicean tendencies?

Let the text speak as the text, and let's have enough of creating theories to support the whims and fancies of the end-time speculators. Let us rather seek to honour Christ and his suffering people. If you really feel that *your* church is Laodicean, do something about it! But don't drag other faithful and suffering brothers and sisters into the mire of your own self-descriptions. And if you really are concerned about being Laodicean, the remedy might be more simple than you think:

Do not be afraid, little flock, for your Father has been pleased to give you the kingdom. Sell your possessions and give to the poor. Provide purses for yourselves that will not wear out, a treasure in heaven that will not be exhausted, where no thief comes near and no moth destroys. For where your treasure is, there your heart will be also. (Luke 12:32-34)

SEVEN

The glory of the Lamb
Revelation chapters 4 and 5

Chapter 7

The glory of the Lamb
Revelation chapters 4 and 5

As you approach this section, I strongly recommend that you take the time to read the two chapters, and if at all possible, read them out loud. Let the words and the sounds of the words fill your mind and your ears, just as they would have done for the believers two thousand years ago in a small, persecuted church in a regional city in Asia Minor. Read out loud so that you hear what they heard. Let the majesty of the vision wash over your soul.

As you read or hear the words, what is your overall impression? Forget the details and the desire to try and work out why the creatures have four faces or who the twenty-four elders are. Stick with the overall impression. What impresses you about these descriptions?

In these two chapters, we are eavesdropping on the ceaseless worship of God and of the Lamb. At the centre of all things are the One who sits on the throne and the Lamb. Every creature from every level of the created order is there before the throne, along with all the blood-bought saints of all the ages. Unnumbered beings, from heaven and earth, are singing the praises of the one who inhabits eternity and the priceless Son who loved us and gave himself for us.

If we aren't able to suggest an actual explanation for every detail, it still goes directly to our hearts. Remember, it is a vision. John was taken into a realm where no human being has ever been, and he saw things that must be utterly beyond human language. Human beings think in pictures. We use metaphors and images when literal descriptions don't go to the heart. Our proverbs are metaphors. Our most common expressions are metaphors. When things are beyond description, when scientific analysis or statistical calculations cannot touch the nature of what we see, we use metaphors. Try describing a magnificent sunrise, or a terrible storm, or strong emotions without using similes, metaphors and images. Waves crash like thunder; skies catch on fire; stars are diamonds; waters are like crystal. We have a fire in our belly; a chill in our soul.

In human communication, it is the images and comparisons that give the richness of understanding to what we see. So, too, with John. Let's allow him to use great images and metaphors to convey the immeasurable power of the vision he sees, without trying to turn him into a scientist. Just enjoy the vision!

The purpose of the chapters

The role of these chapters is to establish an essential foundation for all that follows. Throughout the remainder of the book, we will see the ongoing battle between the dragon and the followers of the Lamb. We will be compelled to think about the terrible conditions on earth and our human frailty. As we read of the terrors of life on earth and what successive political and religious regimes have done and are doing to the saints, we need to know that above and beyond every power, every authority, every scheme of the enemy, there is an absolute power, and absolute authority. We need to know that his is the victory now and eternally, not just in the future. We need to know that all of history follows his plan and that he is the one under whose authority it unfolds. John's visions may move us into scenes of battles and struggles, but the Lamb has *already* won and has *already* ransomed a people for himself.

These chapters are necessary as the foundational antidote to fear.

Some interesting sights and sounds

Obviously, the major detail of the two chapters, the one that leads us ahead into the rest of the book, is the scroll with its seals and the Lamb opening it. However, before we get to that, there are a few characters upon whom people like to dwell. The twenty-four elders for example, who or what are they? Some feel they may be the two foundational twelves – the twelve patriarchs and the twelve apostles. That is not unreasonable, but we must note that John is one of the twelve and yet he is watching them. So, after a little thought, perhaps that doesn't work as well as might first appear. Some feel they represent the churches of the Old and New Testaments. But in glory we do not need to be represented; we are there, among the numberless throng. We have had one representative, Jesus, our "forerunner", as Hebrews 6:20 says.

Perhaps a better question is whether or not we actually *need* to know who the elders are, and whether an explanation is actually warranted. Perhaps a secondary question would be what significance that knowledge would play in the vision or in our lives. What if we do not know, or cannot decide? What have we lost? Nothing! The vision remains and is still overwhelming in its magnificence and power. So if we cannot decide, what might we say about them? Simply this: in heaven there is authority, there is rule, order and structure, just as in God's Kingdom on earth.

God has his angels, his archangels; is he not also able to have twenty-four elders to do his bidding if he wishes? And those who administer and rule as elders worship the Lamb more fervently than all. They cast their crowns, their status and authority before him, preferring to have no honour in his sight, but to give every honour, every title, even that which they themselves possess, to him for his glory. It is a scene of the supremacy of the Lamb. To wear ourselves out on secondary issues and images is to miss the glory of that vision.

The four living creatures? I have read some interesting speculation about their four faces, with thoughts about the face of the lion being for kingly authority, the ox for strength, the eagle for speed, the man for wisdom and intelligence. In other words, these represent the greatest strengths of the created order. Again, that may be reasonable, but is it helpful or necessary? Is it suggested by the passage itself? Or the rest of Scripture? The point is not to dismiss the elements of the vision, but to diminish our Western passion for turning everything into a scientific or statistical statement. To excessively analyse and accurately describe things that are in glory before the throne is not something we are capable of doing satisfactorily, because we can only work within our existing framework of knowledge and experience. In fact, God the Father is described as sitting on the throne. Do we imagine that God has a bottom? That he has a physical body that bends in the middle where his legs join his abdomen? The point is that none of this vision responds well to scientific analysis, so don't bother trying. Simply relax in the sure knowledge of the power that rests with God alone, and the confidence that everything in heaven and earth is bent to his glorious, eternal will. He is the absolute centre.

Why does God have seven spirits? Let me say again, simple is best. Later we read that Jesus has seven eyes, and we don't really figure that into our literal reckoning of what Jesus looks like. So maybe, in our simplicity, we can see that there are seven churches written to, each of which has the Spirit in it, and each of which is under the watchful eye of Christ – seven and seven.

What about the sea of crystal? I once read the confident assertion that this represents all the nations of the earth – but again, why? Why must it represent anything at all? In the Old Testament, before anyone entered the temple or tabernacle, they saw a huge bronze basin called the "sea", used for the washing and cleansing of the priests. We don't make it represent anything; it just is what it is. In the heavenly tabernacle we also see a "sea", but this one is not bronze, it is as pure as crystal. And it is what it is. Enjoy the vision!

With any visions of the dwelling place of God, or of God himself, there will be things beyond our comprehension; things that work best for our hearts if we step back from them and allow them to go beyond our scientific and statistical mental processes.[20] We see immeasurable authority and strength, we see living creatures unlike any other in the created order and yet, in some ways, like all others. We see thrones, authorities and order, and most significantly we see everything in heaven and on earth, every level and every structure praising the one who sits on the throne and the Lamb. And among them all, whether they be elders or powerful creatures or angels or men, there is none worthy to open the scroll except the Lion, who is the Lamb.

The Lion of Judah

Way back in Genesis 49 when Jacob was blessing his sons, inspired by the Spirit of God, he made a prophecy about each one and the tribes that would ensue from them. When Jacob came to his son Judah, he said,

---

20   This in no way implies anti-intellectualism! Nor does it imply that the Scriptures are incapable of satisfying our intellects. But some things are best left in the realm of the heart, especially with apocalyptic literature such as this. Would your marriage be enhanced if you could analyse and describe the biochemistry of romance? Or if you tried to make every term of endearment – "baby, sweetheart, honey" – into a literal statement?

"Judah, your brothers will praise you; your hand will be on the neck of your enemies; your father's sons will bow down to you. You are a lion's cub, O Judah; you return from the prey, my son. Like a lion he crouches and lies down, like a lioness – who dares to rouse him? The sceptre will not depart from Judah, nor the ruler's staff from between his feet, until he comes to whom it belongs and the obedience of the nations is his." (Genesis 49:8-11)

Someone would come from Judah who would be a king and whose rule would be like a lion. Rouse him up and you will pay the price, just as if you had toyed with a lion. To him the ruler's sceptre would belong, and he would come and claim it. In other words, he would be the true king, the one to whom that sceptre rightly belonged.[21]

That promise remained in the hearts and minds of Israel as they awaited their king. Indeed, the coming of the King and the Kingdom are perhaps the greatest of all underlying themes in Scripture, tying God's Word together for us from beginning to end. Those twin expectations, the King and the Kingdom, are like the great themes of a symphony that rise and fall through the various movements, but are always there. After the failures of each successive king, the establishment of a true and lasting kingdom seemed impossible. The things David could not achieve continued to slip irretrievably beyond the grasp of Israel with each successive reign, until that remarkable day when John the Baptist burst into Palestine announcing the dawn of the Kingdom: "Repent, for the Kingdom of Heaven is near!" (Matthew 3:2)

---

21   Some English versions have the phrase, "until Shiloh comes". The original Hebrew could be a word meaning "peace", ie until peace, or the one of peace, comes. Or it could be read as a word meaning "whose it is" or "whose right it is". Both are possible. The NIV, and many other versions, use this latter reading, because it was favoured by the Septuagint. Hence the translation, "until he comes to whom it belongs".

As the reins of proclamation moved from John to Jesus, Jesus himself preached the Gospel – good news – of the arrival of the Kingdom of God. He did the things the King would do when he came. He taught about Kingdom living. He was crucified as a king, and even Pilate, a gentile governor, inscribed on the cross for all the world to see: "Jesus of Nazareth, King of the Jews" (John 19:19b).

What was not fulfilled in King David because of his human weakness, nor in Solomon because of his idolatry, nor in any of the kings who followed, would not be fulfilled until, in the words of Jacob's prophecy, "he comes to whom it belongs". We now know him as Jesus of Nazareth, Son of David, King of Israel, King of Kings and Lord of Lords.

But how did this Lion of a King conquer his mighty enemies? As a Lamb! Such is the might and majesty and wisdom of God. As 1 Corinthians says, even "the foolishness of God is wiser than men" (1:25a). None of the rulers of this age – neither the kings of earth nor Satan and his hosts – understood this wisdom of God (1 Corinthians 2:8). Jesus conquered the dragon, not as a warrior but as a lamb, and he redeemed fallen men and women making them "a kingdom of priests to serve his God and Father" (chapter 1:6).

Here is the centre of our scene. Here is the one worthy to open the scroll. He is worthy because of the work of the cross. Therefore, whatever follows is dependent upon that victorious work of Christ. Whatever follows is because of the Gospel.

And the scroll?

To work out what the scroll actually is, the very best idea is to allow Jesus to open it and to look with him at what comes from it. Then we may be able to decide.

EIGHT

The scroll and its seals
Revelation chapter 6

Chapter 8

The scroll and its seals
Revelation chapter 6

We will first look through the seals and then come back to try and fit them into our "big picture" understanding of what they are about and what Jesus is showing us. The first four seals are four horse riders, each of whom is given a task to perform and the authority to perform it.

The First Seal

We see a rider on a white horse. Is it Jesus? That question is sometimes asked because later in the book (chapter 19) we read of the rider on the white horse. The rider of chapter 19 is unmistakeably Jesus. In that later section, he is named King of Kings and Lord of Lords, he has the two-edged sword in his mouth and a robe dipped in blood. There is no mistaking who is being spoken about in chapter 19, but a comparison will show that the rider we meet here in chapter 6 is very different. The rider in chapter 6 does not have authority but is given authority. He rides out to conquer, whereas Jesus has already conquered. He has a bow in his hand, not a sword in his mouth. The more we compare the two, the less it seems possible that they are the same person.

The rider on the white horse here in chapter 6 is one of a foursome, each of whom has a gruesome task to perform, and each of whom only has part authority, not all authority. He is styled like a military conqueror, and his task is to go out to conquer and rule the earth. Has there ever been a time in history when there has been an *absence* of rulers trying to conquer surrounding nations? Has there ever been a time when the leader of one nation or another has not set his mind on expanding his empire by conquest of other nations? The most casual reading of history will show that this world is dipped in blood. Every generation has produced megalomaniacs bent on conquest and slaughtering untold millions in their wake. The history of earth is a history of empires, established with weapons not ideas, most of whose history has been written in blood.

The Second Seal

This rider is permitted to take peace from the earth. He does not actually slay men but allows men to slay each other. Wars, civil wars, murder . . . all these follow in the wake of this rider, for that is the one responsibility with which he is charged. To any observer, the history of our world's politics is a mystery – why so much blood? Civil wars erupt around matters both great and trivial – petty rulers, political infighting – and suddenly men are killing each other. An empire topples and out come the knives as people vie for ascendency. Men kill each other for religious reasons as easily as political reasons, and never seem to see the irony of their actions as they defend their supposedly omnipotent gods with swords of steel. Indeed, peace has been taken from the earth.

The Third Seal

Here we have a black horse whose rider brings scarcity and famine. The prices of basic foodstuffs – wheat and barley – rocket to terrible levels for the poor. A whole day's wages would not buy enough to feed a family, and yet luxury goods, the oils and wines of the rich, are not touched. Throughout history, there has always been famine in one part of the globe or another, while all along there have been the rich, whose supply of life's luxuries has been maintained. Even today, with our immense abilities for food production and distribution, millions starve to death. Daily, children enter the realm of death with wizened bodies and sunken eyes, while in the West we go on weight reduction programmes for sheer excess of food.

The Fourth Seal

Here we see the results of the other seals. This rider is pale, the ghostly colour of death. His name is Death, and that is what he produces, by sword, famine and plague. In the other seals, the authority was given to afflict the earth; here their consequences follow them. Death and the grave are the ultimate winners of every struggle and all political aggression.

None of these riders indicate a universal catastrophe. Just a fourth of the world is killed. Death and destruction are found in various parts of the earth throughout history, but life persists. Death is the ultimate statistic, for it touches one hundred percent of humanity, but many enter the grave ahead of time as politics and nature combine to bring famines. People die in bloody conquests, by disease and by plagues. But life clings to the planet. No disaster is great enough to fill the grave to its capacity.

"A fourth of the earth" is not a scientific number, because this is apocalyptic literature, but the picture is clear. Always there is death, if not here then there, if not today then tomorrow, if not in this nation then in that nation. But never the whole earth.

The Fifth Seal

The fifth seal shows us that believers are caught up in the strife, often as its victims. Death is meted out upon the followers of Jesus by regime after regime. But what we also see is that death is not the end; it is not loss but victory. The martyred saints are waiting under the altar. Again this is an image that is helpful for us. It was customary in the Old Testament for the blood of the sacrifice to be poured under the altar (Leviticus 4:7). Here we see that the sacrifice is the people who have been faithful to Jesus to the point of death.

These martyred saints ask how long it will be until their vindication comes and judgement is meted out against those who dwell on the earth. We are shown that this judgement will surely come, but not yet. More are yet to be added to the number of those who have given their lives for the sake of Jesus.

The Sixth Seal

The sixth seal describes the end. It is unmistakeably clear that the final day of God's wrath has come. Look carefully at what is described for us. Every person on earth, from every level of society, sees "the face of him who sits on the throne" (verse 16). They are fully aware and are terrified of what they see and of the wrath of the Lamb. The earth is shaken, the islands and mountains flee away, the stars fall from the sky.[22] It is over. It is finished. Wrath

---

[22] Remember we are dealing with apocalyptic images. The stars don't really fall to the earth. Just one star, the sun, would burn everyone to death by the time it had scarcely begun its journey. The sun and most other stars are bigger than the earth, some thousands of times bigger, and they outnumber the earth by billions upon billions. But we get the point – everything is finished!

and judgement have come. Here we have the final and great day of the wrath of God, that day of vengeance for which the souls under the altar have been crying out. It is now, at this time of the sixth seal, that the kings and generals – and indeed every human being, from the highest to the lowest – recognise that the one they crucified, the one they now see on the throne, is their judge and executioner.

We have now arrived at the second coming of Christ: the day of the wrath of God, the day of vengeance and judgement. I am emphasising this because it must affect our understanding of the structure and message of the remainder of this wonderful book. At this point in the book, the world is at an end, and there has been nothing secret about the re-entry of Christ into history. It is a very visible, very fearful coming, when everyone on earth sees the Father and the Son – and we are only in chapter 6! The only two conclusions we might reach, based on this, are that either the rest of the book happens after the end of the world, or that the book of Revelation is not a linear series of events.[23]

We still have one more seal to go, and although we do now know when the six seals end, the lingering question will be: when do they begin?

As we think about this, it is important to ask the obvious: is there anything in the text of this book so far to suggest that these seals represent only the last seven years of history – a seven-year tribulation period? The answer is obvious and easy: no. There is nothing to indicate that they represent only the last seven years of history. (We are not saying that it is not possible, only that at this point the Bible does not say so.) The theory of a seven-year time frame must be *brought into* chapter 6; it does not come from *within* the chapter.

---

23 In Chapter 3, under the heading "The Layout or Structure", we also noted that the end of all things is spoken of in the same words in Revelation 17. This is a further confirmation that Revelation does not have a simple linear, or chronological, structure.

In the absence of a starting point for the seals being given here, any schedule of time we arrive at will obviously need to be found elsewhere. We cannot just make something up and call it true.

What Jesus said about these things

The easiest place to look is the teaching Jesus gave to his disciples about the flow of history and the end of all things in Matthew 24. The Matthew passage is important because it is the one place where Jesus clearly answers the question about the sequence and timing of the end. Therefore, it will be important to examine the text of Matthew 24 to see what Jesus really does say, not just to presume we know what is there.

> Jesus left the temple and was walking away when his disciples came up to him to call his attention to its buildings. "Do you see all these things?" he asked. "I tell you the truth, not one stone here will be left on another; every one will be thrown down". As Jesus was sitting on the Mount of Olives, the disciples came to him privately. "Tell us," they said, "when will this happen, and what will be the sign of your coming and of the end of the age?" (Matthew 24:1-3)

Gazing on the beauty of the temple, the disciples have been stunned by the words of Jesus that not one stone will be left standing on another. Here they are with the one they now recognise as the Messiah, the Saviour and King of Israel, and he is telling them that the centre of their worship, the focus of their whole religious life, will be utterly destroyed! So they press him for more information. They ask two questions, or one question in two parts. The disciples probably saw it as one question because, now that Messiah had come, it would have been impossible for them, as Kingdom-oriented Jews, to imagine that the destruction of the temple could be anything other than the end of the world. However, in reality, what they ask forms two questions because, as Jesus will show them, the destruction of the temple and the second coming are two entirely different events at two entirely different times. Their questions are, "When will this [the destruction of the temple to which he had referred] happen?" and "What will be the sign of your coming and of the end of the age?" (We now know that one has already happened and one is yet to happen.)

Jesus knows what lies ahead for these men and for the Jewish nation, and his mind leaps to the warning: "Watch out that no one deceives you" (Matthew 24:4). That is his concern. It is most important, when interpreting a document, to begin with the intent of the writer or speaker. Here, in that sentence, is Jesus' intent. His goal, in giving the details that follow, is that they will not be deceived by anyone or anything. In what way might they be deceived? Look at what he points to. (Can I suggest that you really do read the text? I know that many of us skim over the text when it is quoted in books like this, but so much wild speculation is born of misreading Jesus' words, that to actually take the time to see what he did say is very important.)

> Jesus answered: "Watch out that no one deceives you. For many will come in my name, claiming, 'I am the Christ,' and will deceive many. You will hear of wars and rumours of wars, but see to it that you are not alarmed. Such things must happen, but the end is still to come. Nation will rise against nation, and kingdom against kingdom. There will be famines and earthquakes in various places. All these are the beginning of birth-pains." (Matthew 24:4-8)

There will be false Christs. Perhaps we feel unlikely to be deceived by that, but many groups throughout history have packed their bags and sat on headlands, or on the Hill of Megiddo (Armageddon), or on the outskirts of Jerusalem and so on, because

Jesus was there or about to come there. This happened as recently as the turn of this century when large numbers of believers gathered at Meggido (Armageddon), and many others did all sorts equally foolish things, because Jesus was, or soon would be, arriving there.[24]

Jesus urged them *not* to be deceived by false claims, nor by wars and rumours of wars. There will indeed be wars and talk of wars, but please note the point that Jesus is making about all this: these are *not* signs of the end! Look carefully at what he said: "Watch out that no one deceives you . . . the end is still to come." So many, many people use the worn-out phrase "wars and rumours of wars" to point to the fact that we are now near the end. But Jesus *expressly* says these are *not* signs of the end – "the end is not yet". His point is exactly the opposite! It is that these things will continue to happen all through history. Expect them. Don't be deceived into thinking the end has come. Nations will *always* be at war, kingdoms will *always* be at war, famines and earthquakes will follow *throughout* history, but these are *not* signs of the end. That is what Jesus said. It may not be what a lot of scary, popular literature says, but it *is* what Jesus said.

His illustration of birth pains is helpful. When the pain begins, we know one thing – a baby will be born. We don't know if it will be in one hour, ten hours or twenty hours! We only know with certainty that the baby will come. It is a brilliant illustration because, once the final stage of pregnancy is reached, nothing will stop the baby coming. Yes, the end is certain, but wars, famines, uprisings and earthquakes are not signs of its timing, only of

---

[24] I am referring to the utterly unbelievable panic many Christians experienced because someone said a computer virus, the infamous Y-2K bug, would bring about Armageddon and other calamities. I believe these reactions among believers are a direct result of the foolish speculations that have arisen around Revelation. Christ and his people have not been well served by such foolishness and the proliferation of scary books and movies!

its certainty. Those "pains" must continue until the end – the "birth".[25]

What will happen to believers? Are they to be safe from such earthly events? No, we will also share in the pain, as the unbelieving world that rejected Jesus pours out its rejection of him onto us.

> Then you will be handed over to be persecuted and put to death . . . hated by all nations . . . many will turn away from the faith . . . many false prophets will appear and deceive many people . . . he who stands firm to the end will be saved. (Matthew 24:9-13)

All these things will happen but are not signs of the end. The plan of God for the earth will continue! The timing of earth's history is related to one thing only:

> And this gospel of the kingdom will be preached in the whole world as a testimony to all nations, and then the end will come. (Matthew 24:14)

There *will* be men and women from every nation before the throne on that great day. The promise made to Abraham and reiterated throughout the prophets *will* be accomplished. Then, and only then, the end will come. God keeps his promises and fulfils his purposes.

Why does Jesus tell the disciples these things in answer to their question? Because they are about to experience a time of trouble such as Israel has never yet experienced. They will see the temple of God in Jerusalem utterly destroyed by the Romans, just as Daniel prophesied. And, as Luke includes, Jerusalem will be surrounded by armies. History records that it happened! Please

---

25 In Romans 8:22, Paul reminds us that the whole of creation is and has been groaning with labour pains, awaiting the final revealing of the sons of God.

note that. It *happened*. After a history of rebellion, sedition, and the atrocious acts of the Zealots in the city and in the temple, the patience of Rome finally gave out and they acted. And oh, how they acted![26] First came the terrible siege in which parents even resorted to cannibalising their own children as Rome tried to starve out the population. Then, finally, into the city came the Roman legions, crushing everything in their wake! Josephus, a historian living at the time, tells us that over a million Jews were slaughtered.[27]

Think about the emotional effect of three thousand people dying on 9/11 in New York, a city of many millions of inhabitants. Now think about one million people dying in first-century Jerusalem, a city whose population was barely a fraction of New York's. Think about the slaughter of several hundred children and teachers in the school siege in Beslan, North Ossetia, at the hands of Chechen rebels and compare it to a million people being hacked to death in one small walled city, and you will gain some impression of the shock and magnitude of the slaughter.

Every death was a death by sword or crucifixion or decapitation. That is, up close and personal! The blood of a million

---

26   There are those who speak with great authority on exactly what the "abomination that causes desolation" was. But opinions vary and must vary because we were not there and cannot fully appreciate the nature of events. Was it Antiochus Epiphanes? The timing does not seem to work. Was it Rome itself? Very likely, as they entered and tore down, stone by stone, the place reserved for the high priests of God alone, grinding the blood of a thousand sacrifices under the feet of their Roman sandals. Was there another specific action? What we do know is that those who lived at the time would know exactly what was happening and were well able to heed the warning Jesus gave.

27   Numbers vary. However, even though Jerusalem's population was usually way below that number, Josephus may well be close to the mark because many had gathered in the city for the feasts. Additionally, many from the surrounding countryside had come to the city for refuge. What safer place could there be than God's holy city? They thought they were reckoning with Rome, however, as people who had rejected the Christ, they had failed to reckon with the wrath of God.

people flowed in the streets, accompanied by the agonising death-cries of a million people run through with two-edge blades or nailed to gruesome crosses. The heart of the city was the temple, and Roman legionaries dared to enter that Holy Place and raze it to the ground. "Not one stone here will be left on another . . ." just as Jesus had said (Matthew 24:2b). Where once the voice of the high priest alone was heard, and the blood of the sacrifice was poured out, there was now the blasphemy of bloodthirsty Roman soldiers as they ogled, smashed, and doubtless pocketed the wealth of that (previously) most sacred room on earth.

It must have seemed like the end of the world! Even in Rome itself, the impact was felt, and for her actions, the empire seemed to shudder and sway.

"Watch out that no one deceives you," (Matthew 24:4). Imagine the depth of emotion in Jesus' voice. He knew what was about to happen as he poured out his heart to these men and those who would hear them. "These things are not signs of the end. Don't just stay in Jerusalem looking up as if it is my return!

Get out! Run! Don't even stop to pack a bag!" What he foresaw was the sweeping away of national Israel from its land and the ultimate destruction of their temple as foretold by the prophets. The final harvest of their rejection of Jesus as Messiah would soon be upon them. As Isaiah had foretold, their arrogant "covenant with death" had been annulled and they were to be swept into eternity.[28]

The new cornerstone had been laid, and a new building would be built; not a building of stones but one of "living stones". The old

---

28 In Isaiah 28, God points Israel to her destruction; the time when the new cornerstone will be laid, and she will be swept away. The people refused to believe the prophet, thinking that they had a "covenant with death" – in other words, death won't touch us! But God said that their "covenant", that ridiculous notion of being immune from wrath and destruction, will be annulled and they will be wiped off the earth. That is what happened at the hands of Rome. To this day, the temple is in ruins.

temple made of stones is still in ruins two thousand years later. The new temple, God's people, is growing daily with living stones gathered from every tribe, every tongue, every people and every nation.[29]

So how will the disciples know when it is the end? They will know in the same way that every man, woman and child on earth will know. In verse 27, Jesus tells them *exactly* what it will be like when he comes again. Please note what he *actually* says and the order of events as he describes them.

> For as lightning that comes from the east is visible even in the west, so will be the coming of the Son of Man. Wherever there is a carcass, there the vultures will gather. Immediately after the distress of those days "the sun will be darkened, and the moon will not give its light; the stars will fall from the sky, and the heavenly bodies will be shaken". At that time, the sign of the Son of Man will appear in the sky, and all the nations of the earth will mourn. They will see the Son of Man coming on the clouds of the sky, with power and great glory. And he will send his angels with a loud trumpet call, and they will gather his elect from the four winds, from one end of the heavens to the other. (Matthew 24:27-31)

One thing is certain – there is nothing *secret* about the coming of Jesus! What he says is that when he comes *everyone* will see him and *at that time* he will sound the trumpet and gather the elect. This is what Jesus actually says. He will come *once,* both to end all things and to gather his elect. Not twice. No secret disappearances of aeroplane pilots and drivers of cars. That works well in movies

---

[29] And don't forget that the "all nations" includes Israel. On the day of Pentecost, 3,000 Jews were saved. A few weeks later, the number had reached 5,000. The Gospel was taken all over the world by Jews. As Paul wrote to the Romans, "I ask then: Did God reject his people? By no means! I am an Israelite myself, a descendant of Abraham, from the tribe of Benjamin. God did not reject his people, whom he foreknew" (11:1-2a). It would be worth reading all of Romans 9-11 as you consider this point.

and scary books, but listen to what Jesus said. Please, *listen to Jesus!* Read the verses again. Look at the order of the events . . .

He will come like lightning.

Everyone on earth will see him.

The stars will fall from the sky. (Remember Revelation 6 and the sixth seal?)

People of earth will wail and mourn.

Then the trumpet will sound and the elect will be gathered.

His coming, like lightning from the east to the west, when everyone sees him, will be the time of his gathering of his elect with the trumpet call. As Thessalonians says, the *trumpet* will sound, there will be the *mighty shout* of the archangel, the Lord will issue a *loud command,* and we will be caught up to meet him in the air. And that definitely does *not* sound like a secret![30]

He tells the disciples these things so that they will not be deceived by people telling them that the wars and rumours of wars are signs of the end. Were they to think that the impending destruction of Jerusalem (or wars and earthquakes and famines) signalled the end, they may not take his advice and run from Jerusalem. When the end does come, they will know, as will every man, woman and child on earth. And they won't have to run! They will be gathered to Jesus at the sounding of the trumpet.

If you think about the warnings from verse 15 onwards, they can hardly apply to the second coming, because for us that will

---

30 Some will point to Matthew 24:36-41 as a secret rapture. Here Jesus is speaking about the coming of the Son of Man, and he has already described that event as like "lightning from the east to the west". His point in this section is that, just as in Noah's day, when life carried on as normal, so it will in the days prior to his coming. Two men will be in the field; one will be taken and the other left. Two women will be grinding with a hand mill; one will be taken and the other left. To make it a secret coming *prior* to his real coming confuses the text. He has said as clearly as anyone can, that when he comes, everyone will see him. The believers are still on earth because the trumpet has not yet sounded. And when everyone does see him, life on earth will not continue! It will be finished.

not be a time to run away but to rejoice. The second coming of Jesus is not a time to decide whether or not to pack a bag, because we will not need a bag! No, the section deals with the destruction of Jerusalem – an historic event, the evidence of which is still before us today. In this whole section, there is not even a hint of a secret coming for believers. In fact, Jesus says the opposite, plainly giving us the order of events. He comes, all the people of earth see him and wail in terror, *then* we are taken. It is the end.

The parallels

We are going back over the words of Jesus in Matthew 24 in detail because people do not actually read what Jesus said, but rather adopt a theory that does not come from the passage itself. They then take that theory to Revelation 6 (or vice versa) and completely miss the point of the warnings and instruction we are given in both Matthew and Revelation. Revelation 6 has its parallels in Matthew 24. Did you notice them as we went through the chapters? (I have set the two chapters side by side at the end of this chapter and highlighted some of the points of comparison.)

In both chapters, we see wars on the earth, famines, men killing each other. We see that believers are put to death. In Revelation 6 we see their souls in heaven and are told that more are yet to join them. We see everyone on earth terrified at the faces of him who sits on the throne and the Lamb. The end has come.

What we are shown in Revelation 6

Remember that, in the sixth seal, we have been given the end of the sequence – the Day of Wrath. However, in the description of the seals in Revelation 6, we are not shown the beginning of the sequence. So, by comparing Revelation 6 with what Jesus said when he was specifically asked about the subject, we see he told us that the things we see in the seven seals are the events of history, not just a collection of events covering seven years or so at the end of history. And haven't we seen these things?

Louis Armstrong sang that beautiful song, "What a Wonderful World". And it is – depending on when and where you live. Throughout history, not all men and women have lived in a "wonderful world" – that is just the romance of those of us who happen to live in a season of peace and prosperity. While Louis Armstrong's song still wafts on Western airwaves, people are being butchered, starved and tortured. Children are torn from their parents' arms, or orphaned and left to live on the streets. The forty to sixty million Russians killed under Stalin did not go to their graves singing, "What a Wonderful World". Those tortured or frozen to death in the Siberian slave labour camps were not doing so to the sounds of romantic Western music. The Irish families left to starve to death by the British in the Irish potato "famine" of 1845 and beyond, were not concentrating on the beauties of nature. For them, the "babies cry" of Armstrong's song would have been cries of starvation.

The estimated two thousand Muslim and Hindu families slaughtered in violent race riots in Gujurat in 2002, and the more than four-thousand Sikhs butchered or burned to death in New Delhi just a couple of decades back, were victims of a world from which peace has been removed. China's sixty million who died under one of the world's greatest butchers, Mao Tse-Tung, experienced all the horrors of the four horsemen. And who can speak with true understanding of the pain and anguish of Native Americans, or Indigenous Australians, or the South American nations, as those given "power to conquer" came and shook the foundations of their lives.

In my own life's experience, I have stood in the desert in Sudan and watched people starve to death, children literally dying at my feet while I could do nothing to prevent it. I have walked the streets of one of the world's largest slums, in Kenya, seeing and smelling the filth of the open sewers and drains in which tens of thousands of children live and play. I spent time with friends who live in the region of Beslan, North Ossetia, where in 2004 the bloody school massacre took place. I have walked among the terrible effects of leprosy in India and wondered how on earth I would live with no hands or feet. If I might change just one word of Louis Armstrong's song, "I think to myself, it's a *troubled* world".

All through history, the earth has suffered from men who have been *given* authority to conquer. How could Lenin enslave an entire continent and bind it into such terror? How could Stalin, a Georgian peasant, so dominate Russia that he could slaughter upwards of forty million people? How could one Chinese peasant, Mao Tse-Tung, take over and enslave all of China, killing tens of millions of people and bringing about the worst famine in human history? What about Hitler, or Pol Pot, or the Ottoman Turks and their slaughter of up to 1.5 million Armenians? The answer, as described in the first seal, is that authority was given to them, authority to conquer and kill. Was this just a twentieth century phenomenon? Run your mind back through some names you might know – Genghis Khan, Tamerlaine, right back to the Roman Empire of John's day. Think of the husbands, wives and children ripped from their homelands by American and British slave traders, and chained into a life of brutality beyond comprehension. Think of entire civilisations destroyed by the Spanish, Dutch and British in their feverish empire-building days. Consider the indescribable bestiality of the Japanese in Nanking.

All through history, untold millions have been killed as peace has been taken from the earth. Is the earth at peace now? Over the last few short years, we have seen fighting in Chechnya, Afghanistan, Iraq, across Africa, in Israel and Gaza, in many Latin American countries, in Sri Lanka – wars and wars and wars. As I write these things, in Darfur in Sudan there is terrible suffering and death from a famine nurtured by political hatred and racism. Tens of thousands of men, women and children are being slaughtered by political regimes using nature to create genocide. And yet I have had breakfast, I am sitting in peace looking over green hills, and am listening to Beethoven as I write.

It was only five or six lifetimes ago that over 15% of the entire population of London died of the plague. It was less than two lifetimes ago that forty million people worldwide died of influenza. Yes, God has sent the four riders into the earth throughout human history and a "fourth of the population" – never the whole world at one time, just a portion – is slaughtered. In one season of history here, in another season there – but still man has not seen his foolishness and repented.

As we saw, the fifth seal shows us that the chaos in humanity has also turned towards the believers, and that many will suffer and die for the sake of Christ, just as Jesus said in Matthew 24. Do not think that martyrdom is largely an "early church" phenomenon. Many church historians believe that there were more Christian martyrs in the twentieth century than in all the previous 19 centuries combined! Believers are not exempt. However, through the gateway of death, believers enter rest, not wrath. The martyrs for Christ will lie under the altar and ask, "How long?" Jesus answers, "Wait a little while. More will join you." As Revelation 6 assures us, finally the day of wrath does come and the earth is judged.

What we are being shown in the seals is the flow of history that Jesus spoke of in Matthew chapter 24, but we are seeing it from a heavenly perspective. History is not following its violent course by accident or aberration, it is following its course under the sovereign hand of Jesus who alone is worthy to rule over history. He is the one opening the seals, for he alone has conquered. History is not in the hands of men, or Satan, for even those who work Satan's plans of war, genocide and subjugation of nations are ultimately under a much higher authority than Satan. Satan can act and can move men, but as we see in the book of Job, he is a subject not a ruler. His authority is limited to that which is permitted by "him who sits on the throne and the Lamb".

Although chapter 6 ends here, we have not yet reached the seventh seal. In chapter 7, more is yet to be seen regarding the history of this world.

Additional:

MATTHEW 24 AND REVELATION 6 – A COMPARISON

Matthew 24	Revelation 6
6 *"You will hear of wars and rumours of wars, but see to it that you are not alarmed. Such things must happen, but the end is still to come.*	1 I watched as the Lamb opened the first of the seven seals. Then I heard one of the four living creatures say in a voice like thunder, "Come!"
7 *Nation will rise against nation, and kingdom against kingdom. There will be famines and earthquakes in various places.*	2 I looked, and there before me was a white horse! *Its rider held a bow, and he was given a crown, and he rode out as a conqueror bent on conquest.*
8 All these are the beginning of birth-pains.	
9 *"Then you will be handed over to be persecuted and put to death, and you will be hated by all nations because of me.*	3 When the Lamb opened the second seal, I heard the second living creature say, "Come!"
10 At that time many will turn away from the faith and will betray and hate each other,	4 Then another horse came out, a fiery red one. *Its rider was given power to take peace from the earth and to make men slay each other. To him was given a large sword.*
11 and many false prophets will appear and deceive many people.	5 When the Lamb opened the third seal, I heard the third living creature say, "Come!" I looked, and there before me was *a black horse! Its rider was holding a pair of scales in his hand.*
12 Because of the increase of wickedness, the love of most will grow cold,	
13 but he who stands firm to the end will be saved.	6 Then I heard what sounded like a voice among the four living

14 And this gospel of the kingdom will be preached in the whole world as a testimony to all nations, and then the end will come.

15 "So when you see standing in the holy place 'the abomination that causes desolation', spoken of through the prophet Daniel--let the reader understand--

16 then let those who are in Judea flee to the mountains.

17 Let no one on the roof of his house go down to take anything out of the house.

18 Let no one in the field go back to get his cloak.

19 How dreadful it will be in those days for pregnant women and nursing mothers!

20 Pray that your flight will not take place in winter or on the Sabbath.

21 For then there will be great distress, unequalled from the beginning of the world until now--and never to be equalled again.

22 If those days had not been cut short, no one would survive, but for the sake of the elect those days will be shortened.

23 At that time if anyone says to you, 'Look, here is the Christ!' or, 'There he is!' do not believe it.

creatures, saying, "A quart of wheat for a day's wages, and three quarts of barley for a day's wages, and do not damage the oil and the wine!"

7 When the Lamb opened the fourth seal, I heard the voice of the fourth living creature say, "Come!"

8 I looked, and there before me was a pale horse! Its rider was named Death, and Hades was following close behind him. *They were given power over a fourth of the earth to kill by sword, famine and plague, and by the wild beasts of the earth.*

9 When he opened the fifth seal, *I saw under the altar the souls of those who had been slain because of the word of God and the testimony they had maintained.*

10 They called out in a loud voice, "How long, Sovereign Lord, holy and true, until you judge the inhabitants of the earth and avenge our blood?"

11 Then each of them was given a white robe, and they were told to *wait a little longer, until the number of their fellow-servants and brothers who were to be killed as they had been was completed.*

12 I watched as he opened the sixth seal. There was a great earthquake. The sun turned black

24 For false Christs and false prophets will appear and perform great signs and miracles to deceive even the elect--if that were possible.

25 See, I have told you ahead of time.

26 "So if anyone tells you, 'There he is, out in the desert,' do not go out; or, 'here he is, in the inner rooms,' do not believe it.

27 For as lightning that comes from the east is visible even in the west, so will be the coming of the Son of Man.

28 Wherever there is a carcass, there the vultures will gather.

29 "Immediately after the distress of those days *the sun will be darkened, and the moon will not give its light; the stars will fall from the sky, and the heavenly bodies will be shaken.'*

30 "At that time the sign of the Son of Man will appear in the sky, and all the nations of the earth will mourn. They will see the Son of Man coming on the clouds of the sky, with power and great glory. 31 And he will send his angels with a loud trumpet call, and
 they will gather his elect from the four winds, from one end of the heavens to the other."

(Emphasis added)

like sackcloth made of goat hair, the whole moon turned blood red,

13 and the stars in the sky fell to earth, as late figs drop from a fig-tree when shaken by a strong wind.

14 The sky receded like a scroll, rolling up, and every mountain and island was removed from its place.

15 Then the kings of the earth, the princes, the generals, the rich, the mighty, and every slave and every free man hid in caves and among the rocks of the mountains.

16 They called to the mountains and the rocks, "Fall on us and hide us from the face of him who sits on the throne and from the wrath of the Lamb!

17 For the great day of their wrath has come, and who can stand?"

(Emphasis added)

NINE

The Gospel at work
Revelation chapter 7

Chapter 9

The Gospel at work
Revelation chapter 7

Having reached the sixth seal, we are shown another aspect of God's work before we reach the seventh. This is a recognisable pattern of this book. In future sections, we will see the same pattern of six things, followed by something apparently outside and alongside the flow of those six things, then the seventh.

In this instance, having seen the terrible turmoil on the earth, we are given a glimpse of the work of God in the Gospel as he fulfils his promise to Abraham. The wonderful, glorious, message of this chapter is that the turmoil of human history does not and cannot prevent God gathering to himself a numberless multitude from every nation on earth. God keeps his promises! People from every tribe and nation are seen before the throne. This chapter is one for rejoicing.

"After this, I saw . . ."

Let me remind you that John begins chapter 7 with the words "After this, I saw . . ." As noted earlier, in our six keys to interpretation (see chapter 3), it is important to notice what John actually writes. He does not say, "The next thing that happened was . . ." He says, "After this I saw . . ." Those are two very different things. One speaks of the chronology of the event. It tells us what *happened* next. The other speaks of the order in which he *saw* things.

Were I to wander through a museum, I might well see things from many different eras and ages, but not necessarily in the order they occurred. I could write about my experiences in two different ways. One would be to organise everything I saw into its chronological sequence and write it as an historical journey. The other would be to unfold the museum to you as I saw it, in the order in which I wandered through the rooms. In the first instance, I would say, "The next thing that happened was . . ." In the second, I would say, "The next thing I saw was . . ." In the latter case, if you misread what I said, you would come up with a very strange view of history!

Understanding this is so important to the interpretation. If we think we are reading a linear progression of time, we will make John say, "After this, this happened." But that is not what he says. And *the proof* is at the end of the previous chapter, where John has already shown us the end of all things – the destruction of the earth and the revealing of the Father and Son to all people on earth.

The subject of the chapter

In chapter 7, the subject is the sealing of the servants of God. We are told that history will not be brought to the final conclusion spoken of in chapter 6:12-17 until the servants of God are sealed. Simply put, while there is a terrible situation on earth as mankind suffers continually under the universal consequences of sin and the Fall, the great redeeming work of God continues. Just as chapter 6 is about the shape and character of an unbelieving world throughout history, chapter 7 is about the work of redemption throughout history. The end will not come until the full number of the redeemed are gathered in. However, because of the unusual way the numbers work and the groups are described, those of us who are not born and bred in a culture attuned to apocalyptic literature need to pause and work out who is being spoken about and what actually happens to them.

In this chapter, we meet the 144,000 of verses 4-8, and the numberless throng of verses 9-10. Who are they?

In verse 3, we are told who the 144,000 are. They are described as "the servants of God". That is not an uncommon phrase to us. By way of comparison, when Peter tells us we must "live as servants of God", we do not see that as an unusual or exclusive term; it is not a group within a group. We know he means us as believers. Nor do we give a mysterious wink and a nod when Paul speaks of believers being "sealed". We are sealed with the Holy Spirit, who is the guarantee of our inheritance.[31] God sealing his servants is neither strange nor indicative of any exclusive sort of group. All believers are God's servants, and all believers are sealed with the Spirit. So the action of God here in sealing his servants is not unusual. What is highly unusual is that here they are described as twelve thousand from each of the twelve tribes of Israel.

The first thing to notice is that the list of tribes is not strictly correct. It is *not* an accurate list of the twelve tribes.[32] God knows who the tribes are, so why give us a modified list here? Always remember we are dealing with apocalyptic literature and it is the very nature of the literature not to deal in scientific or statistical information. So perhaps the actual names of the tribes are not the issue. Rather, the issue is that God's servants are sealed – the whole Israel of God.[33]

---

31   2 Corinthians 1:22; Ephesians 1:13; Ephesians 4:30

32   Joseph is mentioned and yet the twelve tribes include Joseph's two sons Manasseh and Ephraim, not Joseph. While Manasseh is mentioned, Ephraim is not; neither is Dan. Additionally, the list begins with Judah, the tribe from which Jesus came, not Reuben, the oldest.

33   Throughout Revelation, the number twelve and multiples of twelve are often used. Indeed throughout scripture, we see twelve as being a complete

(To know the exact number of those to be saved from your clan or tribe would be intolerable for humanity. What if you knew that exactly 7,000 people from your city or suburb were to be saved – and no more? How would you handle that information? The Yahweh's Witnesses made this terrible mistake and it has made them a laughingstock ever since. Don't be like them.)

There is an incident in chapters 4 and 5 that may help us in the process of interpretation. In that section John saw a scroll that no one was able to open. He wept because of it, but was then told something remarkable. He heard that the Lion of the Tribe of Judah had conquered – and was worthy. He heard about the Lion who would come from Judah as the true ruler, a Jewish expectation since Genesis 49. He *heard* about the Lion, but when he turned he *saw* a Lamb. This was not what he expected to see. It went against the Jewish expectation of a mighty conqueror.

Perhaps here in chapter 7, we see the same pattern. John *hears* of twelve thousand from each of the twelve tribes. And before he has time to work out that the list of tribes is incorrect, or to work out that probably far more than a hundred and forty-four thousand Jews had *already* believed in Jesus, he looks and *sees* a great multitude that no one can number from every tribe, tongue, people and nation. Here is the great and glorious fulfilment of the promise made to Abraham. That promise was *never* made exclusively to or for national Israel, but was *always* intended for all nations on earth in Jesus. National Israel was only ever the womb through which Messiah would be born. God's purpose was

---

number. Twelve tribes, twelve apostles, the dimensions of the New Jerusalem are 12,000 x 12,000 x 12,000 and so on. No one can suggest that exactly 12,000 Israelites are saved from every tribe any more than they might suggest the New Jerusalem is 12,000 stadia (2,200 kilometres) high. In fact, when we get to chapter 21, we will see that the city is not a city at all, but is the bride, which is the people. We are God's city, God's dwelling place. Revelation is apocalyptic literature in which the message is built upon images not statistics. Literal reading was never intended for this form of literature.

always that salvation would reach the ends of the earth. And it has! A numberless throng has been washed in the blood of the Lamb! From Jews and Gentiles, God has created one new nation, the new Israel, "the Israel of God". (Galatians 6:16)

We have already seen the great multi-national throng of believers in chapter 5. What is shown to us in this section is that same numberless throng from every nation in relation to the troubled flow of human history. History proceeds – wars, famines, earthquakes, conquerors – and so too does the Gospel. It is exactly as Jesus told the disciples: "This Gospel of the Kingdom will be preached . . . to all nations and then the end will come" (Matthew 24:14). So the Angel has said in 7:3, "Do not harm the earth until . . ." And when the number is complete, and the Gospel has borne fruit in every nation, then the earth will be harmed and the day of God's wrath will come.

Some additional reading

I have included Ephesians 2:11-22 below because it is such an important passage in this regard. It is so often forgotten by people who try to distinguish between Israel and the Gentiles in relation to the Gospel. The division, or dividing wall, has gone forever! There is now only one new nation. Nothing could be clearer:

> *Therefore, remember that formerly you who are Gentiles by birth* and called "uncircumcised" by those who call themselves "the circumcision" (that done in the body by the hands of men) – remember that at that time you were separate from Christ, excluded from citizenship in Israel and foreigners to the covenants of the promise, without hope and without God in the world. But now in Christ Jesus you who once were far away have been brought near through the blood of Christ.

> For he himself is our peace, who has *made the two one and has destroyed the barrier,* the dividing wall of hostility, by abolishing in his flesh the law with its commandments and regulations. His purpose was to create in himself *one new man out of the two*, thus making peace, and *in this one body to reconcile both of them to God through the cross,* by which he put to death their hostility.
>
> He came and preached peace to you who were far away and peace to those who were near. For through him we both have access to the Father by one Spirit. *Consequently, you are no longer foreigners and aliens, but fellow-citizens* with God's people and members of God's household, built on the foundation of the apostles and prophets, with Christ Jesus himself as the chief cornerstone. In him the whole building is joined together and rises to become a holy temple in the Lord. And in him *you too are being built together* to become a dwelling in which God lives by his Spirit. (Emphasis added)

What is described by God is one new man, one body, one group of citizens, one new building. Look at John 10, where there is "one flock and one shepherd" (v16). Look at Romans 11, where there is one olive tree. Or 1 Peter 2, where there is one new temple of living stones. If I might interpose some words of Jesus on another subject, "What . . . God has joined together, let not man separate," (Matthew 19:6b, RSV). Don't separate believers into two camps, Israel and the Gentiles. That barrier has been torn down once and for all on the cross (Ephesians 2:14).

Out of the great tribulation

John is asked who these people are, and as a good diplomat, he throws the question back to his questioner. In answer he is told: "These are those who have come out of the great tribulation."

What is being referred to here?

It is hard to be unaware of the widely held view that, at the end of this era of history, there will be a seven-year period of unparalleled distress and anguish on the earth, a period called the Great Tribulation. According to this view, believers will be removed from the world before it, and the unbelievers will go through it.[34] Is this what is indicated by the phrase "the great tribulation"?

It is important to remember that this book is a letter. As such, it will follow a logical pattern, and the writer will expect it to be understandable (and applicable) to his readers.

So let me ask you: has there been anything in the text of Revelation *so far* that would indicate that there is one tribulation season lasting seven literal years? The answer is clearly, "No". Up to this point in the letter, no seven-year event called The Great Tribulation has occurred or been mentioned. So if we want to make these two words mean a seven-year period at the end of history, we must bring that meaning into the text, from another place in the Bible, another place in this letter, or from a previously held view.

As sometimes happens with strongly emotive ideas, this is a case where a common word has taken on a life of its own because of the mountain of meaning that has been heaped upon it. So let's work with the word as the first readers would have read or heard it.

The words "great tribulation" mean "great distress" or "great anguish". The Greek word translated as "tribulation" is not uncommon in the New Testament. A brief check of a tool such as Strong's Concordance will show you the 45 places where this word appears in the New Testament, including other parts of Revelation. Sometimes the connections are obscured by our

---

34   I am not trying to be simplistic by this description. I know there are many complexities in that view of the end times. It is simplified here only because of the question we are actually dealing with in relation to the text of Revelation thus far.

English translators' word choices, but with a little bit of digging we discover that, for example, in Revelation 1:9 John says of himself,

> I, John, your brother and companion in the *suffering* [same Greek word – tribulation] and kingdom and patient endurance that are ours in Jesus, was on the island of Patmos because of the word of God and the testimony of Jesus.

That was happening to John and the other believers *at the time when he was writing*. He says of the church in Smyrna,

> I know your *afflictions* [same Greek word – tribulation] and your poverty – yet you are rich! I know the slander of those who say they are Jews and are not, but are a synagogue of Satan. (Chapter 2:9)

So if you had never heard of a tribulation *event* lasting seven years, and simply let the book itself speak to you, what would you have seen?[35] *Up to this point*, you would have seen that John himself (1:9), and the churches to whom John wrote (also see 1:9), especially Smyrna (2:9), have been undergoing terrible torment. You would have read of the flow of history with wars and famines and earthquakes. You would have read of believers being martyred because of their faith in Christ. To comfort them, the first thing they are shown is that history might be in turmoil, but it is Jesus who is in control. Persecution may well be directly meted out against believers, many saints may die as a result, but throughout history, as they come out of the great distress and anguish (tribulation) of the earth, they go to stand before the throne dressed in white. So, "Smyrna, you may be suffering, but you will stand before the throne. The Gospel will not be stopped. Fear not. Hold on. Press on."

---

35   In later chapters, we will meet the period of three and a half years several times, from which the theory of a seven year period is usually derived.

If the flow of the book means anything, then what is referred to is not an event, but a description of what has gone before. Jesus said, "In the world you will have tribulation [same Greek word – tribulation] but I have overcome the world" (John 16:33b). In John 16:21-22, speaking to the disciples as they approached the time of his crucifixion and their terrible sense of loss, Jesus said,

> A woman giving birth to a child has pain because her time has come; but when her baby is born she forgets the anguish [same Greek word – tribulation] because of her joy that a child is born into the world. So with you: Now is your time of grief, but I will see you again and you will rejoice, and no one will take away your joy.

In Revelation 6, we have seen terrible sufferings/tribulation on the earth. We have thought about how those sufferings have gone on and on throughout the history of this fallen, troubled, God-hating world. We have seen the believers caught up in it, and many of them put to death in the most cruel and sadistic ways. And now, at this point in John's visions, he is shown the great multitude of believers who have come out of that long period of tribulation during which Satan and his hosts have waged war against the believers. The value and strategic significance of what John is shown in this section is that the believers have been sealed by God, and nothing can destroy that seal.

We will need to test our thinking on this subject as the rest of the book unfolds. We will see if other passages point us to one seven year period, or a pair of three and a half year periods. However, up to this point, we have not come across any suggestion of a seven year time frame.

It seems therefore that, in keeping with apocalyptic literature's use of numbers as images, the 144,000 – the perfect 12 x 12 number from Israel – is in fact a numberless throng from *every* nation. The promise made to Abraham was always an international promise through which all nations would be blessed.[36] This numberless throng, the worldwide fruit of the work of Christ, has come out of the tribulations of this broken world and into a glorious eternity with Christ. However, suppose we are wrong about the 144,000 and John is actually showing us first the Jewish believers in Jesus and then the Gentile believers, so we know that both Jews and Gentiles who believe enter the presence of God. What changes for us regarding the main message of the book? Nothing. Those who are before the throne are there for one reason only! Whether Jew or Gentile by birth, they have been washed in the blood of Jesus.

The seventh seal

The final verse of the scene is chapter 8:1.[37] Seal 6 covered the end of history, the grand climax. In chapter 7, we have seen that throughout earth's troubled history, men and women have been saved from all nations. So, having come to the end of the world as it is, what comes next? When the seventh seal is opened, there is silence in heaven. Nothing is said and nothing is seen. The history of our world is finished! It is over. Half an hour is a tiny space of time. But it is sufficient for us to get the message! It is sufficient to make us reflect on everything that has gone before. The arguments are over. Judgement has come. Indeed, heaven

---

36   You may find a reading of Romans 9 to 11 helpful.

37   The original book was not written with chapter and verse divisions. These were added much later as a human device to make our navigation around the text of Scripture a little easier. Sometimes the divisions are helpful, sometimes they are unhelpful. This is one of the unhelpful breaks because it prevents us being satisfied that the whole scene is completely finished once the seventh seal has been opened. It makes people want to gather chapter 8 under the seventh seal. However, had those who inserted the divisions made 8:1 the last verse of chapter 7, we would have been content. The scene is well rounded and neatly wrapped up.

and earth are stunned into silence as the God of the whole earth rises to avenge his people and to mete out judgement on the whole earth.

This is not a new concept. What is the key verse of Habakkuk? Habakkuk shows us God as the absolute sovereign, moving nations, judging nations, raising up kings and destroying kings. And Habakkuk 2:20 shouts into time and eternity, "The Lord is in his holy temple, let all the earth keep silent before him!" These words in Habakkuk are not a devotional nicety, they are a command that no man or woman, king or queen can disobey. In his presence, there *will be* absolute silence; no excuses and no explanations. Here now in Revelation, at the end of all history, after the day of God's wrath has come, nothing can be said or done. No pleas can be entered. No enemies can raise their voices. God is sovereign. God has acted. Let all heaven and earth be silent.

Jesus has won the victory

What then is the message, or the impact, of chapters 4, 5, 6 and 7 for a persecuted church in the first century, and for us?

There will never be peace in human history, because God has sent the riders out into the world to remove peace. Death, famine and destruction will be constants in the world. Tribulation will be the way the world is. (History has shown that to be true. Human history is written in blood.) Only Jesus, the Prince of Peace, can bring peace. But throughout the history of the world, God is at work. Through and despite the enemy's work of destruction, God is at work. And just as Jesus said, these wars and famines and military empires are not signs of the end. The end will not come until the full number of the elect is gathered in. God *will* do it. They *will* be sealed. They *will* be kept for all eternity. If you are living in times of persecution and distress, take heart. God is in control.

But this leads us to a question: what is the function of the wars and famines in God's plan? Why is he acting this way? Chapter 8 begins a section that shows us where the purposes of God are heading.

TEN

Let the earth be warned!
Part 1
Revelation chapter 8 and 9

Chapter 10

Let the earth be warned! Part 1
Revelation chapters 8 and 9

We saw at the end of the previous chapter that the seventh seal ends what has gone before. It comes up to, and beyond, the end of history as we know it. That vision is finished. It is time for the trumpets to begin.

Do the trumpets fit chronologically after the seventh seal, or at least after the sixth seal? Here again we see the insurmountable difficulty of trying to make Revelation fit into a timeline in which each scene or section follows chronologically after the one before it. Were that to be so, it would mean that the trumpets come after the end of history, after the earth and sky and stars have been removed, and after every man, woman and child on earth has seen God on his throne. It just doesn't work! What we have in the seven trumpets is a new vision that covers the same ground, but with a different message. The seven trumpets show the same period of history up to the return of Christ, and will proclaim a warning to an unbelieving world. If you doubt that, skip ahead to the seventh trumpet (Revelation 11:15-18), where once again you will see the day of wrath. Once again, you will see the day of judgement and the day for rewarding the saints. Once again, you will see the day for destroying those who have destroyed God's earth. Unless there are multiple days of wrath and judgement, and multiple ends of the world, we must be seeing the same end to which the seals pointed us. The fact that it is also a pattern of seven strengthens the literary link for us.

Before we move into these chapters, let me remind you of the nature of the literature we are reading. Let me take you back in your mind to what we saw in 2 Samuel 22:1-17 as David spoke about God defeating his enemies for him (see chapter 2 of this book). We saw images and symbols, none of which would ever, or could ever, be interpreted literally. Anyone who attempted to develop a theory of the details of God's nose or throat, or bow and arrow would be thought to be utterly foolish. Anybody who searched the details of the battle for the time when the floor of the ocean was bare and dry, and the foundations of the earth visible, would search in vain. David is speaking in hyperbole, or apocalyptic images, and within them he is also drawing on the past. There *was* a time in his forefathers' history when the floor of the sea was laid bare; but of course, David was not there at the time. David's overwhelming understanding is that the same God who delivered Egypt through the Red Sea, turning it into dry land, delivered him in his distress, and David uses that image, among others, to speak of his own deliverance. That is the nature of the literature. To press for literal connections is literary foolishness.

If you are about to approach the trumpets with a Western scientific need to resolve every detail, image and paradox, let me urge you to imagine one of those huge signs often seen on freeway off-ramps, saying, "Go Back. You are going the wrong way." And the wrong way is just as dangerous (theologically) as travelling the wrong way on an off-ramp of a freeway. It has led people to dishonour Christ and the Gospel, albeit unintentionally.

A correct view of God

At this point, it is important to understand that while we might say, "God is warning the earth", it does *not* imply that God is *deliberately* and specifically causing or aiming each hurricane, earthquake, flood and fire! That is a caricature of God sometimes put forward by sincere but misguided believers. The forces of nature were affected when sin entered the world. God is allowing the natural world to follow its destructive course with its resultant effects on mankind. God *can* cause; God *can* prevent; just as he did in Egypt at the time of Moses. But most natural disasters are normal cycles and seasons of the earth. And when a pyromaniac lights a forest fire, it is not God striking the match; it is sin manifest in a broken human being. The world is in chaos, and each event should be a warning to humanity and a reminder of our frailty, perhaps awakening our sense of estrangement from the creator God.

It is also important to remember that Christians die in these events alongside unbelievers. Why? Because, as inhabitants of the earth, we are affected by the natural cycles of the earth. Just as Jesus walked with God in a fallen broken world, becoming tired, hungry, and eventually beaten and crucified, we walk with him in this same, broken world. We live in hope, but have not yet stepped into the consummation of that hope. Our perspective comes from Romans 8:19-25:

> I consider that our present sufferings are not worth comparing with the glory that will be revealed in us. For the creation waits in eager expectation for the children of God to be revealed. For the creation was subjected to frustration, not by its own choice, but by the will of the one who subjected it, in hope that the creation itself will be liberated from its bondage to decay and brought into the freedom and glory of the children of God.
>
> We know that the whole creation has been groaning as in the pains of childbirth right up to the present time. Not only so, but we ourselves, who have the firstfruits of the Spirit, groan inwardly as we wait eagerly for our adoption to sonship, the redemption of our

bodies. For in this hope we were saved. But hope that is seen is no hope at all. Who hopes for what they already have? But if we hope for what we do not yet have, we wait for it patiently.

The scene begins

The scene begins with an angel taking a censer and blending incense with the prayers of the saints. The prayers of the saints and the altar are not new ideas to us. We have come across them a little earlier. In seal 5, we saw an altar with the blood of the saints running down from it. In that scene, the prayer of the saints was a cry for justice and vindication: "How long . . .?" Here now, as the scene of the trumpets begins, we see heaven's altar once again, and this time, just as in the Old Testament, incense is mixed with the prayers of the saints. And just as in the Old Testament tabernacle and temple, these now rise to the throne of God. In that simple image is the link between the seals and the trumpets. God *does* hear the cry of his people and he *does* act, not just at the end, but right throughout history. And throughout history, all his actions are directed towards the great day of justice and wrath, a climax that he alone controls.

The point is in the overall impression and message. As with Israel in Egypt, God has heard the cry of his people. The deliverer will come. He will judge and destroy his enemies, just as he judged the gods of the Egyptians, and will set his people finally, and forever, free.

Today people say that we are at the end, near the second coming, because we now have nuclear bombs that can rain down fire on the earth, or because we now have this or that technology. Now, they say, we can see the prophecy literally fulfilled in a nuclear war or some other modern device. (Have you noticed that it did not seem to bother God, when dealing with Sodom and Gomorrah, that the nuclear bomb had not yet been invented? Or that the absence of biological weapons did not seem to thwart his attack on the Egyptians?) But all through history, men and women have done the same. They have seen the events of their time as being the beginning of the end. They were right, and they were wrong. In actual time frames they were wrong, but in seeing the hand of God and the spiritual conflict behind the events, they were absolutely right.

It is important to recognise how Scripture speaks. We have been living in what the Bible calls "the last days" ever since Calvary. (Take a moment to read Acts 2:17, Hebrews 1:2, Hebrews 9:26 and 1 Peter 1:20.) All through history, we have seen the actions of God on a fallen world, causing chaos and crisis so that mankind might repent. All through history, we have seen men and women tortured for the sake of Christ. All through history, we have seen governments rising up against the people of God.

The first four trumpets show us "cosmic chaos".[38] For humanity, it is the exact opposite of what we see in Genesis prior to the Fall. Before the Fall, mankind lived on the earth and had dominion. Adam[39] was God's ruler, God's vice-regent. The earth was subject to mankind. Now it has been turned upside down. Chaos seems to rule. All of the things that should be secure are insecure. The sky, the earth, the seas and the rivers – all the things created good and for our blessing – become the cause of mass destruction. Instead of being a source of life, they bring death. However, you will notice that through all the chaos – the earthquakes and the terrors of earth, sky and sea – none of the events is totally destructive. Only a third of mankind is killed. The 'third' is not intended to be literal, but indicates partial destruction. (This is not scientific literature.)

The language used in this scene is like the language and concepts used when God delivered his people from Egypt. It is like the language of the prophets who spoke of the first coming of Jesus.

---

38   Paul Barnett, Apocalypse Now and Then, AIO Sydney 1989

39   Please note that God called the man and the woman Adam. This is not a male thing! The man and the woman were two parts of one whole (Genesis 5:2).

Trumpet 1

Are we to think God is actually going to throw blood from the sky onto one third of the earth? I think not. Stay with the genre; this is apocalyptic literature! But we see hail – terrible climatic problems from above. We see fire – terrible destruction from on earth. And we see blood, terrible human devastation. A third of the earth is devastated – but not all.

If, right now, you were to survey the world in which you live, you would see terrible devastation and destruction across the earth. Floods, fires, bloodshed. People are dying in huge numbers *and it has always been so*. A few years ago, there were fires across Indonesia so devastating that, thousands of miles away in other countries, people were wearing gas masks against the smoke and ash. In Australia, there has been great drought. People pray for rain as they always do, and when it comes they forget God and regard the rain as good luck. We have seen huge earthquakes, uncontrollable weather patterns, shocking forest fires . . . At any time, across the world people are dying. Tens of thousands are dying daily – but not all people. Many countries carry on without a care because, at any one time, much of the earth remains untouched while other parts are devastated. So, in the first trumpet, we see that God acts against the earth and environment.

Trumpet 2

God acts against the sea. Terrible destruction! A mountain being cast into the sea – this is an image we are familiar with. Do you remember Daniel's interpretation of Nebuchadnezzar's dream? In his dream a huge rock came and crushed the kingdoms of the earth into fine powder. The rock grew to become a mountain that filled the earth. What was the mountain? The Kingdom of God. It was not a mountain or an atom bomb or a meteor! It was a *symbol* of the mighty, spiritual work of God.

Revelation uses images and metaphors the same way. Here in the second trumpet we have an image of God acting, through which we also get a glimpse of his wrath. The mountain is hurled against the sea, and both natural and commercial disasters result. At the end of 2004, we had a tsunami that caused unimaginable, instantaneous death, and focused the minds of the world on the frailty of life – for a few moments. But then life went on.[40] In 2005, Hurricane Katrina all but wiped New Orleans off the face of the earth. The authorities began to drain the waters from the city, and then Hurricane Rita came and repeated the destruction. Year after year, there are massive and destructive hurricanes and storms in various parts of the world and people blame God. People shake their fists at heaven and ask why. "If there is a God, why . . .?" The answer is: "Because there *is* a God; that's why!" And yet, so few turn and repent and seek mercy from the God of creation.

Trumpet 3

The star Wormwood – is it a real star with poisonous gasses? A comet? The name Wormwood means bitterness. Here God strikes the inland waterways, the primary resources of life on earth,

---

[40] In all this, it is imperative that we recall the words of Jesus in Luke 13:1-5, "Now there were some present at that time who told Jesus about the Galileans whose blood Pilate had mixed with their sacrifices. Jesus answered, 'Do you think that these Galileans were worse sinners than all the other Galileans because they suffered this way? I tell you, no! But unless you repent, you too will all perish. Or those eighteen who died when the tower in Siloam fell on them – do you think they were more guilty than all the others living in Jerusalem? I tell you, no! But unless you repent, you too will all perish.'" The issue is not that some are more guilty than others, but that all have sinned and all need to come to repentance. Ultimately death and judgement will come to all. That it comes more dramatically to some is a warning to others.

and people are in anguish. It is great bitterness. Despite meteors falling into waterways, are rivers today polluted? Do they dry up? Do life-giving rivers now kill people, or withhold their life? Yes. All of these things happen and are happening. No matter what people do, the earth becomes worse. Behind it all, God is acting and causing the anguish and bitterness.

I recall the buzz of excitement as Christians quickly pointed out that "Chernobyl" is Ukranian for "wormwood".[41] Here was a disaster that could be specifically found in Revelation! Or so they wanted us to believe. But is that the only disaster in which thousands of people have been killed? In all of history, is that the only bitterness meted out upon a broken mankind, and on the rivers, streams and pleasant pastures upon which we rely? In India, a massive earthquake killed twenty thousand people, but the name of the town does not mean wormwood. So because many Bible interpreters are intent on the "this equals that" reading of Revelation, they focus on Chernobyl but not on India.

The Great Plague of London was a terrible outbreak of bubonic plague that ravaged the city from late 1664 to early 1666, killing perhaps more than 75,000 of a total population estimated at 460,000. That is a phenomenal per capita death count, being about sixteen percent of the entire population! Following straight on its heels – from September 2-5, 1666 – came the worst fire in London's history. It destroyed a large part of the city including most of the civic buildings, old St Paul's Cathedral, 87 parish churches and about 13,000 houses.

In 1883, the island of Krakatoa erupted in an explosion that defies human comprehension. The sound was heard up to 5,000 kilometres away. Waves 40 metres high dumped 600 ton blocks

---

41   Chernobyl was the worst nuclear accident in history. In addition to the initial death toll, some authorities suggest that around 270,000 cancers have developed in adults and children.

of coral on beaches, as if they were pebbles. Ash fell on ships over 6,000 kilometres away.

In 1908, an asteroid exploded over Siberia. People were knocked unconscious 500 kilometres away! Trees were flattened across a 2,150 square kilometre area. Reindeer herds were reduced to ashes and a farmer's shirt caught fire 125 kilometres away! Such was the heat generated.

Between 1918 and 1920, an influenza pandemic killed an estimated 40 to 50 million people across the world, with some creditable estimates going as high as 100 million! Between three and six percent of the entire population of the earth killed in one pandemic. That is an unimaginable calamity, one all but forgotten as we look with horror on 3,000 people killed on 9/11 in New York.

In 1138 AD, 230,000 people were killed in an earthquake in Syria. A staggering 1,110,000 were killed in an Eastern Mediterranean earthquake in 1201/1202.

And who could forget Pompeii? In 79 AD, Mount Vesuvius erupted, a harbinger of death. Many fled the city, but some remained, only to become a modern tourist attraction, their bodies frozen in agonising death.

It is only our short memory, or ignorance of history, that makes us "now-focused" in relation to these passages in Revelation. Right across the world, and all through history, there have been disasters of incredible magnitude. The world is sick, the world is under the wrath of God (Romans 1:18-32), and people are feeling his wrath all through history. Some repent, many do not.

Trumpet 4

The sky is struck. With each of these trumpets, it is pointless to try and ask exactly *what* and exactly *how*, because this type of (apocalyptic) literature is never interested in such questions. It is concerned with *who* and *why*. The "who" is God – he is the One behind the earth's terrible instability. The "why" is that God is warning the earth. With each trumpet, the destruction and chaos are not complete. Just a third of the earth, a third of the seas, and so on is affected.

The sun, God's great blessing upon the earth. Always there. Always our friend and life-giver. But no. When Krakatoa erupted, huge portions of the world were plunged into darkness. Midday became like night-time.

In Australia, as kids, we used to run and play in the sun from morning until night. It was our playmate. Now, two out of every three Australians who live to age 75 will contract at least one of the forms of skin cancer. Two out of every three! At varying times, in various places, even the sky has become our enemy and executioner.

Trumpet 5

Before the blowing of trumpet five, a severe warning is given to the earth. The world *is* to take this seriously. In the first four trumpets, mankind suffers indirectly – the earth, commerce and so on, are affected. But now they will suffer *directly*.

The fifth angel blows his trumpet and we see a fallen star, a pit, and a horde of locusts who, unlike normal locusts, do not attack the green grass but attack the people. And please note that they were not allowed to touch the people who had the seal of God on their foreheads. This action of God is against unbelievers, not believers. Also note that, at this time, the believers are still living on the earth. Nothing in this book, so far, has even begun to suggest that all believers have been removed prior to these events occurring.

We do not expect a literal pit opening up in the earth with literal locusts. No one with any familiarity with apocalyptic literature would expect a hole to open in the earth, with sulphur smoke arising and hordes of locusts with faces like people, and golden crowns on their heads, and hair like women and so on. Nor are these beings described as humans, but are creatures that torment humans. The overwhelming impression is that we are witnessing evil spirits, Satan's great hordes, wreaking havoc upon the lives of people. Like Satan, they prowl the earth and create chaos and destruction. Their appearance is like women, or like men, or fearsome animals, or war-horses, or kings – any and every imaginable appearance. But their sting is the sting of death. People will long for death to escape the misery they inflict, but it will not come.

Having read how God has struck at the earth, now we read how Satan, the fallen star, strikes at mankind. Just as locusts leave fields stripped and bare, so these locusts will leave mankind stripped and bare and longing for death. But death is not in the hand of the evil spirits, or Satan, or men and women. The One who has the power over death and hell is Jesus (see chapter 1 of this book). Wishing for death is not enough. God alone controls our times and our seasons.

As you read this, remember that the sealing of the people of God is not just an end-time process. Every believer was sealed from the day he or she believed; sealed with the precious Holy Spirit, the guarantee of our inheritance. Therefore, while this is happening, there are believers on the earth, men and women who have been sealed by the Spirit of God. Is there anything in the text to suggest that this is a Jewish remnant? No. If there is any consistency in our New Testament, we know we have only one group of people sealed with the seal of God. The seal is for all believers, Jew and gentile alike, because no one will be presentable in God's sight other than through faith in Jesus. As Romans 3:22-24 (for example) so clearly shows us, all have sinned and all alike must come by faith.

All through history, there have been what can only be imagined as terrible demonic attacks on mankind. Kings with the power of demons behind them; philosophers and leaders who have come from nowhere and captured the minds of nations, leading them into the valley of the shadow of death, gripped with fear. We have seen nations erupt in incomprehensible violence, brothers against brothers, neighbours against neighbours. Men and women have been tormented and left longing for death as Satan and his hosts work their evil on the earth.

We are told that they will torment for "five months" – a limited time, an incomplete time. Some suggest that locust plagues usually last five months, not all year, but the effects of such a plague linger for a generation. Here the time span of their attacks is limited by God, as is the scope of their work – only a third of mankind is affected at any one time. A literal third? No more literal than the locusts are literal. A literal five months? No more literal than the third of mankind. What we are seeing is a power that does not destroy all of mankind or affect all of mankind forever, but in seasons, just like locusts.

Remember that freeway sign, "Go Back. You are going the wrong way". In our modern way of thinking, the details need to be explored. We are unsatisfied with a lack of specifics, but that is the wrong way. This is apocalyptic literature. It is the impression that counts.[42] We have seen nature and the powers of darkness create havoc on the earth under God's permissive hand. And in verses 20 and 21 of chapter 9, we are shown the purpose: that those who witness the devastation might repent. But they do not.

Trumpet 6

Four angels are released to do God's bidding. They have been prevented from doing their work until the very day and hour

---

42 To be trying to make the hair of the locusts the vapour trails of fighter planes, and other such fantastic interpretations, is really quite foolish. It actually works against the simplicity and power of the message.

that God determines. The impression seems to be that all the fury and bloodshed of war are released. Two hundred million troops mounted on animals as ugly and ungainly as anything we might imagine. This is unstoppable war, with troops and armour we cannot tame. Those who lived through the world wars will know what an unstoppable beast war is. People fight and die, and die, and die. No matter how loudly we might cry, "Stop!" the tumult of war just rolls on, crushing all in its wake.

Is the 200 million a literal number? So few numbers, if any, in this type of literature, are to be taken literally. Here we have an incalculable number of evil workers in the earth – demons and instruments of evil. But despite all their work, mankind has not come to repent. Look at situations like the former Yugoslavia, or Sudan today, or the French Revolution, or the American Civil War, or Stalinist Russia, or Uganda, or Rwanda. Suddenly there is madness, and men are slaying their neighbours and their family members and committing unbelievable atrocities. What sparked these things? Where did the madness come from? How can a man live at peace with a friend and neighbour for years and then suddenly turn on him and hack him to death with a butcher's knife? How can a nation suddenly be roused to such fury that ordinary men and women are turned into butchers who run death camps in order to slaughter an entire race of people? Where did the insanity come from in the USA when, after three days of fighting at Gettysburg in 1863, up to 51,000 men lay dead or wounded – brothers killing brothers, cousins killing cousins, fathers and sons on opposing sides – and almost every death occurring at point-blank range. How can Russian turn against Russian and slay 40 million through Stalin's era? How? *How*?

In the terms of the seals of chapter 6, a rider has gone out with the power to take peace from the earth. In the terms of these trumpet warnings, the angels have gone out to wreak their havoc. The angels move at the hour, the day, the month and the year that God determines, and their actions destroy a third of mankind – but not all. Will those who remain in Russia repent? Or Yugoslavia? Or Uganda? Or Sudan? Or America? No. The idolatry continues.

ELEVEN

Let the earth be warned!
Part 2
Revelation chapter 10 and 11

Chapter 11

Let the earth be warned! Part 2
Revelation chapters 10 and 11

If we simply read chapters 8 and 9, or better still, hear them read out loud as the initial recipients of the letter did, the movement and drama are breathtaking. Wave upon wave of horror unfolds upon the earth as God allows the events of earth's troubled history to bring an unheeded warning. Probably no century characterises the mood of these chapters more in our minds than the twentieth century. But that is because we are closer to it than any other century. Would facing bloody disembowelling by the Mongol hordes be less terror-filled than facing a twentieth century army? Would facing tortures deliberately created to mimic the fires of hell by Ivan the Terrible in fifteenth century Russia be any better or worse than facing the hellish tortures in Stalin's twentieth century Russia? Would facing the torture of medieval times be any less a fearful prospect than the torture legislated into legitimacy by the Bush administration in the USA? Each century has had its terrors in war, famine, plague and demonic madness.

Trumpet 7

Having swept through the warnings of God, in chapter 10 we come to another interlude. This is the same pattern we have met before – six and then an interlude. During this interlude, in chapter 10:7, John is told that when the seventh trumpet is sounded,

> "... the mystery of God will be accomplished, just as he announced to his servants the prophets."

Whatever is about to happen is not a new message or a new plan. It is an ancient plan, a plan "announced to his servants the prophets" and now fulfilled. And that is exactly what we see. When the seventh angel sounds his trumpet, the mystery of God *is* accomplished. The word "accomplished" means "brought to a close". For a moment, let's step beyond the interlude, and look at the seventh trumpet at the end of chapter 11:

> The seventh angel sounded his trumpet, and there were loud voices in heaven, which said: "The kingdom of the world has become the kingdom of our Lord and of his Christ, and he will reign for ever and ever." And the twenty-four elders, who were seated on their thrones before God, fell on their faces and worshipped God, saying: "We give thanks to you, Lord God Almighty, the One who is and who was, because you have taken your great power and have begun to reign. The nations were angry; and *your wrath has come. The time has come for judging the dead, and for rewarding your servants the prophets and your saints and those who reverence your name, both small and great – and for destroying those who destroy the earth.*" (Chapter 11:15-18, emphasis added)[43]

---

43   "The nations were angry ..." Once again we have a reference to Psalm 2, that great and magnificent challenge by God to the nations of the earth. They have plotted and schemed in vain. God has established his King, and he will reign forever. In Revelation, we see the climax of all that this wonderful Psalm spoke of. Just as the disciples took courage from that Psalm in Acts 4:23-31, so can we. The victory does belong to God's Anointed, no matter what our particular season of history might look like.

Can you see that once again we have come to the end? We have reached the time when there will be "no more delay" (10:6) – literally "no more time". The mystery of God, all that has been planned since eternity and accomplished in Jesus, will be fulfilled and brought to its close. God's enemies are destroyed, and his saints are rewarded.

There are not multiple ends to history! There are not multiple days of wrath, or multiple final judgements. What we are reading about now, we have read about before, and we will read about again. Each new sequence, or series, of visions in this book is overlaid upon the others. Each shows us the work of God through history. Each focuses on a different aspect of that divine work. Each brings us to the end of all things and the day of wrath. The seals in chapter 6 made one major point – the one unfolding history is the Lamb. He is in control. The history of earth will be written in blood and fire, until he brings it to its conclusion. The trumpets show us that same period of history, but we are given a far more dramatic insight. We see that these events, the troubles of earth, are not aimless, nor are men and women without hope. God is warning the earth through dramatic natural, political and permitted demonic activity and allowing time for repentance. We see now in the seventh trumpet that nothing in heaven or earth can stop the mystery of God being accomplished – the mystery that is in, through and for Christ Jesus.[44]

In chapter 6, the end of all things was spoken of in terms of the destruction of the earth and the created order. Here the end is spoken of as judgement. It is the same end – human history only ends once! This again demonstrates that Revelation cannot

---

44   "Mystery" is a strategic word for the apostle Paul as well. He uses it to speak of the Gospel. The work of God in Jesus was in the shadows throughout the Old Testament, a mystery to those who tried to fathom when, and through whom, all the promises of God would be brought to fruition. In Jesus, the mystery is revealed – the mystery was and is Jesus himself. (See Romans 16:5; Ephesians 1:9; 3:3; 3:9; 6:19; Colossians 1:26-27; 2:2; 4:3)

be one sequential time-line. It is an overlapping series of scenes. Otherwise we have multiple second comings, multiple days of judgement and multiple ends. We need to let John's structure determine the chronology. Timelines might look good on wall charts and in scary end-time novels and movies, but they do not fit the text and pattern of what John wrote.

So, in chapter 10:5-7, there is the announcement of the end. The Angel swears by the God of heaven that there will be no more delay. He will act as he is bidden by God and will blow the seventh trumpet. We see that end in chapter 11:15-18. But there is an interlude, something else we need to know.

Chapter 11

We have seen the sequence of the trumpets, with all their drama, concentrated on the work of God against the people of the earth. We have seen their stubborn refusal to repent. But that is not entirely what the history of the earth is about. No indeed! It is also about the work of the Gospel, through which men and women from every tribe, language, people and nation are purchased for God. So it would be incomplete, or too one-sided, and perhaps even too depressing, to think only of destruction. The interlude therefore, brings us the balance. In it, we see the unchallengeable, unstoppable witness of the Gospel throughout that same period of history.

Chapter 11 is difficult because of the nature of the images. It once again confronts our Western way of reading which drives us to make every detail find its place. This is especially so because some of the images are expressed in quite definite terms. We have the temple being measured. We have two witnesses. The Beast makes war on them. However, we also step somewhat outside the easily explainable as we see them breathing fire and calling down plagues. They are also called "olive trees" and "lamp stands".

There are commentators who see all of the things here as being literal. Some see it as a literal temple to be rebuilt after believers have been removed from the earth. A literal altar on which, once again, sacrifices are to be made to God. Literally two witnesses – two men – who, like mythical dragons, breathe out fire and smoke, and who are killed and rise again. Many follow that line of thinking, but consider what some aspects of those interpretations do to Christ!

From the time of the first coming of Jesus, there has been no physical temple. There is no *need* of a temple, and there *never will be* the need of a temple. We now have Jesus. Jesus declared himself to be the temple of God, the dwelling place of God among mankind (John 2:21-22). And, in Christ, the people of God are now the temple of God. Paul has spoken of this in 1 Corinthians 3:16-17; 6:19 and Ephesians 2:21-22. Peter has spoken of it in 1 Peter 2:4-5. What is abundantly clear in our New Testament is that the temple of old was a shadow of that which would come – God dwelling among his people. Its fulfilment would not be in a building but in Jesus of Nazareth, and then in his people by means of the indwelling Spirit. The Spirit of God no longer descends on a physical building for limited periods but indwells God's people forever. As Jesus told the disciples at the Last Supper, the Spirit would be with us and in us forever (John 14:15-17).

The shadow of an earthly temple has been dissolved in the brilliant reality of Christ, the dwelling place of God among men. And now his people – the Church – are being built into the temple of the living God. To approach this passage with any sense of a restoration of physical temples and sacrifices is a complete denial of the reality, Christ, who has eternally fulfilled the shadows.

Jesus is unmistakeably the fulfilment of the temple. He is also the final, once-for-all sacrifice. He is the one true high priest. Those Old Testament shadows of the temple, its sacrifices and priests, are finished for all time and eternity. To reinstate them is like crucifying the Son of God all over again by declaring his first and final sacrifice insufficient, and his embodiment of the Father (Colossians 1:9) inadequate. Always keep in mind the type of literature that Revelation is. By stepping outside the genre, many people dishonour Christ, even though they have no intention of doing so. Let the Gospel determine your interpretation – never contradict the Gospel and the finished work of Christ!

Don't make Israel's mistake

Israel missed her messiah because she was looking for literal things to deal with literal symptoms, whereas God was always speaking of a higher reality. Israel wanted a physical king to destroy their physical enemy, the Romans. They wanted Jerusalem to once again be the great and glorious city, like in David and Solomon's time, with a temple to which all the world might look in astonishment. Perhaps there was a desire to regain or demonstrate superiority.

But because Israel wanted a kingdom in this world, it missed its messiah, whose Kingdom was not of this world. His temple was never going to be a restoration of what Solomon built, for he himself was the dwelling place of God on earth. His Zion was never going to be Jerusalem, for his city would be his people (we see this at the end of Revelation). His Kingdom would never be militaristic, nor would it be geographically centred on the Middle East, for God would make "the ends of the earth your possession" (Psalm 2:8b). The breadth of his rule would be across the whole earth, because it would extend beyond Israel and comprise men and women from every tribe and nation.

That was always the plan. Don't make the same mistake as Israel. Don't be so focused on an earthly city, an earthly people and an earthly temple that you miss the great reality, which is Jesus.

So many of our end-time novelists and speculators have stumbled, just as Israel did, by looking for physical, earthly realities. Like Israel of old, they are in danger of missing the wonder of what God had intended since eternity past. They are so focused on God restoring the "shadows" that already have been fulfilled in Christ, that they are missing what God is doing now. They are missing the awesome power we have now as we reign with Christ, transferring people from the kingdom of darkness to the Kingdom of God's Son. We are conquering the enemy "by the blood of the Lamb and the word of . . . [our] testimony" (chapter 12:11). We are breaking down strongholds through prayer.

The work of redemption in Christ is not now, and never will be, about earthly geography! It is about gathering people out of the earth and into the heavenly city. As Hebrews tells us, we "have not come to a mountain that can be touched" (12:18a).

> But you have come to Mount Zion, to the heavenly Jerusalem, the city of the living God. You have come to thousands upon thousands of angels in joyful assembly, to the church of the firstborn, whose names are written in heaven. You have come to God, the judge of all men, to the spirits of righteous men made perfect, to Jesus the mediator of a new covenant, and to the sprinkled blood that speaks a better word than the blood of Abel. (Hebrews 12:22-24)

Measuring the temple

How then, should we approach this interlude in chapters 10 and 11? What is this portion saying to us? Chapters 10 and 11 bring before us images that are strangely familiar. Ezekiel was asked to measure the temple. Zechariah was asked to measure the Holy City. The two olive trees that stand before the Lord are a direct reference to an incident in Zechariah. Yes, we have met these things before in our Bibles. They are not new images. God is simply drawing them together for us in the revelation of the victory of Jesus, the one in whom all the plans of eternity are brought to completion.

So what do we have? John is asked to do what the prophets Ezekiel and Zechariah before him have done. The action of measuring the temple, or the city, seems to be to set apart that which is inside and holy from that which is outside and unholy. The temple – now the people of God in Christ – has definite limits. Universalism, the idea that everyone is saved whether they know it or not, has no place in the teaching of Scripture. There are defined, identifiable limits to the number of the people of God. God knows those who are his.

Forty-two months

Outside the temple, the holy city will be taken over by the Gentiles "and they will trample the holy city . . ." (chapter 11:2). There is a distinction between the true people of God, the true dwelling place of God, and the outside world of unbelievers. They are to trample it for "forty-two months". That is a figure, or period of time, that we will meet several times in Revelation, and it helps us a very great deal in understanding what we are looking at.

Many will say, "Ah, there are the first three and a half years of the seven year tribulation." But that is not what we are told. No tribulation is mentioned. We are told that the Gentiles, unbelievers, will trample on the city of God for forty-two months. (If you sneak ahead and look at Revelation 19 and 21 you will discover that the *city* of God is, in fact, the *people* of God, an image absolutely consistent with the Gospel and the words of the prophets.)

As we try to work out the forty-two months, we are compelled to see the parallel words of Jesus in Luke 21:20-24, because Jesus uses *exactly* the same words:

"When you see Jerusalem being surrounded by armies, you will know that its desolation is near. Then let those who are in Judea flee to the mountains, let those in the city get out, and let those in the country not enter the city. For this is the time of punishment in fulfilment of all that has been written. How dreadful it will be in those days for pregnant women and nursing mothers! There will be great distress in the land and wrath against this people. They will fall by the sword and will be taken as prisoners to all the nations. *Jerusalem will be trampled on by the Gentiles until the times of the Gentiles are fulfilled."* (Emphasis added)

When will "the times of the Gentiles" begin? The times of the Gentiles began with the fall of Jerusalem. It is not the second coming, because no believers will be required to run and hide in the mountains when Jesus returns! No. Jesus spoke about an historical event. We examined this in chapter 8. It has happened. It was visible. Jerusalem and the temple were forever replaced as the city and dwelling place of God, because Jesus had come. We are no longer gathered to a holy city, or a temple, but to Christ. He was rejected in Israel, and through that rejection, the Gospel has gone to all nations. The destruction of Jerusalem and the temple was so great that Jesus wept openly for what he could see was about to happen. It occurred around 70 AD.

Therefore, what Jesus spoke about began when Jerusalem was surrounded by armies, conquered and trampled on by Gentiles. Therefore, how long has the "time of the Gentiles" been so far? So far, the time of the Gentiles, has been two thousand years; since 70 AD. So, how long has the apocalyptic figure of forty-two months been so far? It is also two thousand years so far. It *is* an apocalyptic image.

Why forty-two months, or three and a half years? Perhaps because it is half of seven. In this book, God's actions relating to his eternal plan are seen in sevens, whereas the times of the apparent rule of unbelievers are only half of seven. Great and powerful as it might seem, the rule of unbelievers falls very far short of God's rule. (We will test this interpretation of the forty-two months when we meet it again in chapter 12. If it is as we have suggested, then it will be a consistent image wherever it appears in this book.)

As described in this chapter, the two witnesses prophesy for the same period of time during which the city of God is trampled on by the Gentiles. How long is that? So far, two thousand years. This tells us that they cannot be two literal men who breathe out of their mouths fire that burns their enemies to death. That is not God's way in any case. We would never imagine that God would create such monsters. More importantly, the terminology is not new to us. Jeremiah was told,

> Therefore this is what the LORD God Almighty says: "Because the people have spoken these words, I will make my words in your mouth a fire and these people the wood it consumes." (Jeremiah 5:14)
>
> "Is not my word like fire," declares the Lord, "and like a hammer that breaks a rock in pieces?" (Jeremiah 23:29)

When we read this, we never imagine Jeremiah as breathing fire on his audience, resulting in them being burned to death on the spot. We don't imagine people with their skulls literally crushed because they have heard Jeremiah speak the words of God. We understand what God is saying. We accept the images. Why then do people persist in requiring literal meanings for these same images when they see them in Revelation? Stay with the genre. Without wishing to seem overly repetitive, it is apocalyptic literature.

There are many facets to these two witnesses, and many connections with the Old Testament and other New Testament images as well. The two witnesses are obviously *styled* after Moses and Elijah. Elijah called down fire from heaven and shut the heavens against rain. Moses afflicted Egypt with plagues. But as we have seen, Jeremiah also spoke fire and consumed the enemies of God.

The witnesses are also described as two candlesticks. What have candlesticks been used to describe earlier in this book? The church.[45] They are also described as two olive trees. Again, we are familiar with the image of an olive tree representing the people of God (Romans 10-11). They are described as standing before the Lord. Even though they are on earth, they stand before the Lord.

They are also closely aligned with Zechariah's vision, in Zechariah 4:

> Then the angel who talked with me returned and wakened me, as a man is wakened from his sleep. He asked me, "What do you see?" I answered, "I see a solid gold lampstand with a bowl at the top and seven lights on it, with seven channels to the lights. Also there are two olive trees by it, one on the right of the bowl and the other on its left." I asked the angel who talked with me, "What are these, my lord?" He answered, "Do you not know what these are?" "No, my lord," I replied. So he said to me, "This is the word of the LORD to Zerubbabel: 'Not by might nor by power, but by my Spirit,' says the LORD Almighty.
>
> "What are you, O mighty mountain? Before Zerubbabel you will become level ground. Then he will bring out the capstone to shouts of 'God bless it! God bless it!'" Then the word of the LORD came to me: "The hands of Zerubbabel have laid the foundation of this temple; his hands will also complete it. Then you will know that the LORD Almighty has sent me to you.
>
> "Who despises the day of small things? Men will rejoice when they see the plumb line in the hand of Zerubbabel. (These seven are

---

45 That it is the same word does not always mean that the image relates to the same reality. However, it can be a guide.

the eyes of the LORD, which range throughout the earth.)" Then I asked the angel, "What are these two olive trees on the right and the left of the lampstand?" Again I asked him, "What are these two olive branches beside the two gold pipes that pour out golden oil?" He replied, "Do you not know what these are?" "No, my lord," I said. So he said, "These are the two who are anointed to serve the Lord of all the earth."

It would be impossible to miss the literary connection between this and what we read about the two witnesses in Revelation. John sees what Zechariah has seen.

So how do we tie all of these multiple images and statements together? What can we possibly make of the two witnesses? How can they be all of these things rolled into one?

The simplest thing to do is answer simply. It was mentioned in the introduction to this book that Revelation is a book of opposites. For everything God does, the enemy has a counterfeit. A few chapters further on, we will read that Satan has his beast and his false prophet. As you read on, you begin to see Satan's beast and false prophet as the religious and political arms of the kingdom of this world. These two strands of Satan's work witness to the corrupt and failing glories of the kingdom of this world. But here in chapter 11, God also has his two witnesses. And his two witnesses *reign* on earth. They are eternally indestructible. While at the end they might appear to have been destroyed, it is a false hope and short-lived joy for the people of earth. God's witnesses rise, ascend to heaven, at which point the accomplishment of all things is announced. The seventh angel sounds his trumpet and the day of judgement arrives. (We looked at this in the previous chapter of this book.)

In that very simple analysis and comparison of opposites, who are the witnesses who remain on earth right through its history, and right through the times of the rule of the Gentiles?

Who ascends to heaven at the very hour that judgement comes? Who rises from the earth on a cloud and joins Jesus in glory? The people of God. The church.

So far, so good – but why two? It is a simple matter of opposites. They are the opposite of the beast (the political kingdom) and the false prophet (the false religions) of Satan's kingdom. They are the kingdom of priests; the people of God functioning in their kingly and priestly roles. (Compare with Exodus 19:6 and 1 Peter 2:9.)

Is that too simple? Satan has his religious and political witnesses on earth, and God has his two witnesses? Satan's two witnesses descend into the lake of fire; God's two witnesses ascend to the presence of God. It is only too simple if we, as Westerners, need to make every detail fit into a tight calculation of exactness. For apocalyptic literature, it is sufficient.

For us, the connections with Zechariah, Moses, Elijah and Jeremiah are unmistakable and yet they are not scientifically accurate, matching detail for detail. Is God not concerned with accuracy? Yes he is, but accuracy is a concept that transcends statistics and scientific formulae. (For example, "I love you with all my heart" can give an unmistakeably accurate *impression*, but is grossly inaccurate medically.) Accuracy of impressions is of far greater significance when thinking through the eternal plan of God and victory of Jesus. *We* want simple theological points with which to construct systems and win arguments. *God* wants our hearts to be stirred and strengthened by things that are ultimately beyond our limited understanding.

Let's look at some of the detail that might lie behind that analysis of who these witnesses are.

Through the prophet Zechariah, God points to his work of building a new temple and a new priesthood on the earth. It is a new building which will have a new capstone. In chapter 3, Joshua the high priest cannot be the ultimate focus, because his life is finite. He must be a symbol, and God says that he is.

> "Listen, O high priest Joshua and your associates seated before you, who are men *symbolic of things to come*: I am going to bring my servant, the Branch. See, the stone I have set in front of Joshua! There are seven eyes on that one stone, and I will engrave an inscription on it," says the LORD Almighty, "and I will remove the sin of this land in a single day." (3:8-9, emphasis added)

God says that Joshua is symbolic of the new priesthood – the cleansed people through whom God would work on the earth. The righteous branch, Jesus, will come. (Note the seven eyes, as in Revelation 5:6. We cannot mistake who the passage is talking about.) This chapter is not about Joshua the man. It is about the things Joshua symbolises – the new priesthood of God at the time when "the Righteous Branch" comes.

Zerubbabel can be seen as symbolic of the new kingly office that would be given to the people of God. Joshua was a high priest. Zerubbabel was a prince of the house of David. Through them, God would work and build a new temple on the earth. That is the background setting of Zechariah chapter 4.

Zechariah then sees two lampstands, or candlesticks, burning brightly with seven channels of the light. But Zechariah also sees the two olive trees and is puzzled by what all this means. The answer is given to him in verse 6 – God will act by his spirit in the earth. Here we have two olive trees perpetually supplying the oil for the candlesticks. And the answer to the puzzle is: *"Not by my might . . . but by my spirit"* (emphasis added). The completion of the new temple and the new priesthood will be by the Spirit of God, not by military might. It will not come about because a military conqueror rescues God's people, but because the Spirit of God is released to work on the earth and rescues people from the kingdom of darkness. The capstone will be set in place. The whole structure will be completed and established.

So again Zechariah asks, "What are the olive trees?" These are the two anointed ones, or suppliers of oil to the candlesticks. These are the means by which the spirit of God will continually supply what is necessary for the church to shine in the world. Who are they then? Are they Joshua and Zerubbabel? If so, then not in person, but in regard to the office or role they fulfilled. They are the priestly office and the kingly/governmental office that God has given to his people – the "kingdom of priests to serve our God" (chapter 5:10; see 1 Peter 2:9-10). In Zechariah, we have the priestly function of the new temple represented by Joshua the priest, and the kingly function represented by Zerubbabel the governor. And they are continually supplied for their task by the Holy Spirit.

Back to John's vision

In his vision, John also sees the two candlesticks and two olive trees before the Lord. These are the two witnesses to God in the earth. They reign with Christ now. They have authority on the earth, supplied by the Holy Spirit of God. Their authority is like Moses; no, it is like Elijah; no, it is like Jeremiah; no, it is like Joshua; no, it is like Zerubbabel . . . no, it is *all* of those rolled into one. Moses withstood the gods of Egypt. Elijah withstood the Baals. The people of Jesus withstand the gods of this age and reign with Christ, overturning empires and tearing down strongholds. In the timing and providence of God, the followers of the Galilean "conquered" the Roman Empire. And in the providence and timing of God, they have risen above each and every successive empire. No empire has *ever* fully shut down the Gospel, and no empire has *ever* taken men and women out of the hand of God. As Jesus said, "No one can snatch them from my hand." (John 10:28)

But what about the calling down of plagues on the earth? Remember our freeway sign! David's descriptions of the victory of God (see chapter 2 of this book) were highly inaccurate scientifically but unmistakably accurate in effect. So too, for the people of God. There are rulers in hell for eternity, kings and emperors, false prophets and demigods, because the people of Jesus have withstood them and prayed against them.

If Scripture comments on Scripture, then the link between Zechariah and Revelation is unmistakeable. In Zechariah, the candlesticks are not two individuals, although they are typified by Joshua and Zerubbabel. Nor in Revelation need they be two individuals, just as at the beginning of the book we see Jesus among the candlesticks – the churches.

They will prophesy throughout the days of the Gentiles, those same forty-two months, starting from the destruction of Jerusalem *as Jesus said,* and lasting until just before the end. That time frame has already been given to us.

And at the end, in a last and great stand against the people of God, the world may well think it has annihilated the people of God. In successive ages, numbers of empires have sought to accomplish this Stalin's Russia and Mao's China, to name just two – but the church has risen again, stronger than ever. This is the first indication in Revelation that there will be a time near the end when the enemies of the Gospel will greatly increase their determination to destroy the Lord's people, unlike anything before. Paul spoke of the rebellion that will occur as the man of lawlessness comes (2 Thessalonians 2:3). Jesus also spoke of it. And we will read more of it later in this book.

The people of God are killed in the city – described here as Sodom, Egypt, and Jerusalem. Egypt was always the great enslaving, oppressive, political power and was utterly humiliated in the plagues of Moses' time. Jerusalem – the religious city, defiant of God to the point of killing the saviour – was destroyed and its people scattered across the globe in 70 AD. Sodom was the great immoral city that raised its fist in defiance of God's created order and was burned to a crisp in a moment of his wrath. Perhaps in this triple naming of the city, we see the whole system of the world that was against God and in which Jesus was crucified. The moral, political and religious rebellion of mankind against God, rises to the point of destroying the people of God, or so they think. All the world sees it, because all the world is involved.

But after the moment of rejoicing, they will gaze in horror as the people of God rise again. The church not only comes back to life, like its Master, but rises like him on a cloud and enters the glory of its Lord. There will be great fear at the fact that God's people are not destroyed, but have returned to life and victory. And then, immediately, the end will come. This is the timetable we saw in Matthew 24. *At that hour* the seventh trumpet is blown and the end comes. *At that hour* the kingdom of this world becomes the Kingdom of our Lord and of his Christ. *At that hour* the time for the dead to be judged "came" – past tense. Not in a future time at the end of another seven years or three and a half years, but at that hour when the people of God entered glory.

In the scheme of this book, it has happened. Once again, we have reached the end. The church has been caught up, the judgement has come. It is not another end, but *the* end – the one single and terrifying (for God's enemies) end of history.

However, there is more yet to be seen. We need to know what happens to the kingdoms of this world. What happens to Satan? What happens to the believers? And so more scenes are overlaid, one upon the other, to complete our understanding.

TWELVE

The Son, the serpent and the saints

Revelation chapters 11:19 to 12:17

Chapter 12

The Son, the serpent and the saints
Revelation chapters 11:19 to 12:17

The next scene we are to witness seems most reasonably to commence in chapter 11:19. In chapter 11:18, the sequence of the trumpets has ended. The trumpets were warnings of judgements on the people of earth. They came. Verse 19 begins a new vision:

> Then God's temple in heaven was opened, and within his temple was seen the ark of his covenant. And there came flashes of lightning, rumblings, peals of thunder, an earthquake and a severe hailstorm. (Chapter 11:19)

The statement paints a very dramatic backdrop for the vision that follows. In that verse, we see the things that accompanied the presence of God on Sinai – lightning, thunder and the ground shaking. These Old Testament images and connections are important to recognise. We are going to read of Satan and his work against the Christ and the believers. But above all of Satan's fury and activity, above every plan he may try to fulfil, is the Eternal One. God has not changed. The authority and majesty we saw on Sinai remains. It has not been, and will not be, challenged or changed by anything the ancient serpent might do.

In chapter 12:1-6, we meet the main characters in this new scene. We have the woman, the dragon and the child. It is perhaps important to note that the woman and the dragon are described as "wondrous signs" whereas the child is not. It seems we are being shown that it is not a literal dragon and not a literal woman, but that the child is very real. So who are they all?

In verse 9, the dragon is explained beyond doubt. We have no difficulty in knowing who or what it is.

> The great dragon was hurled down – that ancient serpent called the devil, or Satan, who leads the whole world astray.

The child is also clearly identified in verse 5. There is only one child who has been taken up to God and the throne, and who will "rule all the nations with an iron sceptre". It is the same child mentioned in Psalm 2, from which the words are quoted. In that Psalm, he is identified as none other than the Son of God.

In this drama, the dragon hates the woman because she is the mother of the child. It is really the child he hates and would devour if he could. But he is unable to destroy the child. Instead, the child is caught up to heaven and the throne, from where he will rule the nations. So far, the image is clear. It shows us something of the drama in the heavenly realms behind the birth of a baby in a small Palestinian town, two thousand years ago. It was a drama that touched eternity.

Who then is the woman? A quick reaction may be "Mary", but the actual experience of Mary cannot be understood in the terms spoken of here. Let's look at some of the indicators. The woman here has a crown with twelve stars in it, just like Joseph's dream. In Joseph's dream the eleven stars were his brothers, the patriarchs of Israel (Genesis 37:9). In verse 17, the ongoing offspring of the woman are "those who obey the commandments, and hold to the testimony of Jesus". These things cannot be said of Mary. She is not our mother, and we are not her offspring.

Here we have an image of a woman giving birth to a child, and thereafter, to all those who have believed in Jesus. Which woman, or which "womb" could possibly be said to be the connection between Jesus and all of those who believe in him? There is only one "woman" – or line – from which we can be said to come, and from which Jesus also came: the true line of Abraham, true Israel.

The woman is the people of God from whom Messiah came forth. True Israel – the people of the promise – was the womb that bore him. We also are born from and into that line when we believe in Jesus. "Those who believe are children of Abraham" (Galatians 3:7). The woman cannot just be *natural* Israel, for we as believers are not in any sense the offspring of natural Israel. We are the *true* offspring of Abraham's line, his children, and "heirs according to the promise" (Galatians 3:29b; see also Romans 4).

The woman continues on for the period of time that we have met before – 1260 days, or three and a half years. This further identifies what that time period is. So, let's consider the figure.

In this drama, when did the 1260 days begin? It began when the child was caught up to heaven. When was that? The resurrection and ascension of Jesus was two thousand years ago. So how long is this apocalyptic image of 1260 days, or three and a half years? It is two thousand years, so far. (This further confirms that the two witnesses in chapter 11 are witnesses throughout the whole history of the church, until Jesus comes again.) No single person, and no group of people, gave birth to Jesus and only lived three and a half years! Nor did Jesus ascend to the throne three and a half years before the end of history! To read seven-year tribulations into these numbers is to impose onto the text what is utterly impossible. These numbers are images. And they are not difficult to work out.

What then is the purpose of this vision? What does God want us to see? It is about the unseen battle. Behind the pain and persecution we might experience here on earth, we have an enemy, the ancient serpent, who was unable to destroy the Christ and so wages war against his people. What about the desert as a place for the woman? It is simply an image drawn from Old Testament history, bringing the church into a parallel experience with the people of Israel in their wilderness journey. They were on a journey, surrounded by enemies, before entering into their final inheritance. And they were kept all the way through by the gracious provision of God. So, too, are the New Testament people of God. In the wilderness, the people of Israel were not yet "home", and neither are we. In Exodus, God used the image of his people being brought to him on eagle's wings, and all the might of the Egyptian army could not reach them or destroy them.

Here in Revelation, the woman is given an eagle's wings to fly into the desert. "Eagle's wings" (chapter 12:14) and being cared for in the wilderness are images that unite us with God's Old Testament people.

> "You yourselves have seen what I did to Egypt, and how I carried you on eagles' wings and brought you to myself." (Exodus 19:4)

His mighty acts of deliverance, his carrying his people on eagles' wings to a place of safety, are the same for us as they were for the Old Testament people of God. This world is no more our home than was the wilderness their home or their final destination. As they were provided for in the wilderness with a foretaste of that which was to come (manna), so are we. Meanwhile the battle constantly rages against the people of God, and obviously we are not always physically safe. Many have given their lives for Christ. But the manna never fails. The water from the rock never runs dry. And we *will* one day cross that river to enter into the land promised to our forefathers. There we will enter God's rest for all eternity. For now we feel the wrath of the ancient serpent. Knowing he could not destroy the child, Satan wages war against the people who hold to the testimony of Jesus. It is a battle outside time, waged in eternity, and yet it affects us in time as the purposes of God are worked out in human history.

The chapter gives us the background to the dragon and how he came to be on the earth to devour the child. It shows the battle in eternity in which Michael, the champion of God's people, fought against the dragon and won. The serpent lost. There was no longer any place for him in heaven. His position with God was also lost. Any claim he may have had to a position of authority was gone forever. The dragon and his followers were cast out of the realms for which they were created. And with the description of their utter humiliation and defeat, comes the great announcement about the Kingdom of God (verses 10-12). The child of Isaiah's prophecy has been born (Isaiah 9:6-7). He will reign forever. Satan was utterly defeated and eternally cast out through the life, death, resurrection and ascension of the child. While thinking he destroyed the child on the cross, Satan actually engineered his own defeat. All authority was given to the child in heaven and on earth and for all eternity.[46]

And the people of God – the other offspring of the woman – may be killed but are not eternally conquered by the dragon. Rather, they conquer him by the blood of the child, the spotless Lamb of God. Their simple testimony about the reality of Jesus is enough to defeat the ancient serpent at every level.

This is wonderful news! The serpent cannot win at any level. He could not defeat Michael. He could not devour the child. Nor can he devour the other offspring of the woman. The people of God are cared for during their time in the wilderness. In fury, the serpent vomits a river of destruction after the woman, but he cannot win. The earth swallows his river of destruction as surely

---

46   Luke 10:18; John 12:31-32; Matthew 12:25-28; Matthew 28:19-20.

as the Red Sea swallowed the armies of Egypt. He is defeated in his desires again and again.

Chapter 12 is a wonderful chapter of victory. Despite the intensity of the drama, and the bitter hatred of the dragon, Jesus has already won the victory. The people of God are secured in Christ. They may suffer as the dragon wages war against them throughout the history of the church – those 1260 days – but they cannot be conquered. We have become conquerors, or as Paul says, "more than conquerors" (Romans 8:37) through him who loved us.

We have read that the dragon, Satan, makes war against the saints, and that his activity is also a "woe" to the earth. But *how* does he make war? Is there anything we need to know that might help us? Yes, there is. And that is the question dealt with by the next vision.

THIRTEEN

The dragon's war
Revelation chapters 13:1 to 14:20

Chapter 13

The dragon's war
Revelation chapters 13:1 to 14:20

In this section, we are going to see something very simple and yet very important. The war the dragon wages is in and through the structures of society, politically and religiously. Put another way, behind the religious and political empires of the world is the unmistakeable hand of Satan. Through those empires, as history so powerfully records, his war is waged against believers. Like two horrendous beasts, the political and religious empires have formed a giant pincer movement aimed at cutting off the Lord's people. But as you read this section, remember what we have already seen – the kingdom of this world has become the Kingdom of our Lord and of his Christ. The child has ascended. Jesus reigns. Jesus wins.

First Vision: The political empires of this world – chapter 13:1-10

First, we are shown the political kingdoms of the world. We see a huge beast come out of the sea. Unlike the Lamb, this beast is grotesque in its appearance. The Lamb is perfect in balance, seven horns and seven eyes, everything in harmony with the task he has humbled himself to perform. His eyes are the very Spirit of God.

The beast from the sea is unbalanced with more horns than heads, and blasphemy written all over them. It is not difficult to work out what we are being shown because this is not a new concept or image for us. In Daniel's day (Daniel 7) the beasts represented kingdoms. If we allow our Old Testament to be our apocalyptic guide, we see that the beast here is not one person, but many kingdoms.

But why only one beast? Because what is now revealed is that many empires, many kingdoms and many political systems, all make up the one ugly beast – the kingdom of this world. Each nationalistic group has thought that its nation was superior, perhaps even a master race. But in reality, they are all attached to the same beast and each is just one of its appendages.

In Daniel's vision, the lion, bear and leopard were separate kingdoms, but here now the kingdoms are all rolled into one. It is one kingdom exercising universal dominion over the people of earth, through whatever political form it takes, in whatever period of history. It has horns (power and authority) and crowns (regimes and empires). These are the rulers of the earth, in the successive nations and empires that have come and gone throughout the times of the Gentiles. They are actually the physical manifestation of the dragon's power on earth. Satan does not wage war on the saints in an abstract sense, but through the regimes that arise to persecute and oppress. He does not bind the people of earth in darkness by issues of personal morality alone, but exercises power over the very nations in which they live. He is the unbelieving world's great puppet master, the power behind the throne.

Satan will exercise power against the believers through the kings and empires of earth for forty-two months or 1260 days. There we have that same period of time. It began with the ascension of the child (as we saw in Revelation 12) and continues until the end. In 13:4, we see clearly that men worship the dragon *through* the empires of this world, not even realising who the real power behind the throne is. The Roman empire of John's day, the Mongol empires, the Ottoman empire, the British Empire, the Third Reich, America today – men and women think their empire's invincible. "Who is like the beast? Who can make war against him?" (Verse 4) But behind the beast is the dragon, receiving all the worship himself.

In John's day, the beast was the Roman empire. It exercised dominion and total authority. It may have seemed like it received a mortal blow with the suicide of Nero. He had set about destroying the believers in terrible persecutions, but he committed suicide. Even the Roman senate declared that Nero's memory should be damned, such was the evil pit into which they saw Rome had fallen. It must have seemed like Rome was shamed and silenced. But then Domitian came to power and revived the persecution of believers even more ferociously. Everywhere, people worshipped the emperor – "Caesar is Lord". Men worshipped the dragon by means of the empire, offering worship to (and through) the Roman emperor. And so it has been throughout history, as empires and dictatorships have come and gone. Even today, in the West, many believers worship democracy, imagining that the combined will of all the people in a country – the godly and the ungodly – adds up to righteousness. How often we hear the sentiment that if we can just get democracy into this country or that, all will be well. It is no different from Israel thinking that if only they had a king all would be well (1 Samuel 8).

Democracy may be a good system for some, but the world will never be free while its true King is rejected![47] Without Christ, all

---

47   In the West, it is hard for us to imagine that our democratic systems are anything but benign, but an honest reading of history shows that the world is not easily divided into "goodies and baddies". Our democratic histories have been histories of national self-interest riding roughshod over the needs of the poorer, vulnerable nations. Democracy does have the potential for all the "good people" to bring about change for the good, but it equally has the potential for all that is evil to come to power. The point is not the system, because a benign dictator

will never be well, because outside of Christ, the kingdom of this world is the playground of the dragon. If believers can be tricked into thinking that freedom and righteousness can be delivered by a political system without God, then the dragon receives his praise, and the line between the Kingdom of God and the kingdom of this world is blurred.

In verse 7, we see that the beast fought and prevailed against the saints, perhaps especially near the end of history. We also saw this in chapter 11. But note verse 8. His authority only extended to those whose names were not written in the book of life since before the foundation of the world. Over those whose names *were* in the book of life, he had *no* authority. In his battle he may *seem* to conquer them. Believers are thrown into prison, martyred, exiled – the voice of the church all but silenced. But over their eternal destiny, the dragon has *no* authority. God reigns! His Kingdom is above all! Daniel saw it clearly:

> In my vision at night I looked, and there before me was one like a son of man, coming with the clouds of heaven. He approached the Ancient of Days and was led into his presence. He was given authority, glory and sovereign power; all peoples, nations and men of every language worshipped him. His dominion is an everlasting dominion that will not pass away, and his kingdom is one that will never be destroyed. (Daniel 7:13-14)

The beast is nothing compared to the Son of Man. The beast only ever has dependent authority. But his warring against us is a call to endurance (verse 10).

Next, we are shown the religious empires of the world arraigned against the Lord and his people.

---

can do as much, or more, good than an immoral democracy. The point is that, outside of Christ, no system is benign or worthy of worship. All systems, outside of Christ, are attached to the beast.

Second Vision: The religious empires of this world – chapter 13:11-13

The beast from the earth looks like a lamb, but sounds like a dragon. That is, it looks like Jesus, but does not sound like Jesus. What looks like Jesus but is really a dragon in disguise? False religions and false ideologies. And that is what the vision of this second beast reveals to us. It makes men worship the kingdoms of this world as it deceives with false miracles and powerful phenomena.

And the people of the earth have indeed been deceived time and time again. Think of Mao in China. He was a mere peasant and yet rose to the point where people worshipped him as a god as he ushered in the economic and cultural "miracles" of a new China. In reality, tens of millions died and more starved to death than under any other regime in history. Was it religious or political? Lenin was the same. Was his system religious or political? This phenomenon goes right back to the Roman Empire where Caesar was worshipped as a god.

We see in John's vision and in history that the two beasts, the religious and the political, work hand in hand, the false religions and ideologies giving life (verse 15) to the kingdoms of the world. They were centred in a person who breathed and was worshipped. Today the Orthodox Church and the state are working hand in hand in Russia to defeat the evangelical believers. Is Orthodoxy a religious or political empire? Is Islam a religious or political system? Is the desire in India for a Hindu State religious or political? Was Soviet communism a political or religious empire? Was Christendom, and empires of the church throughout the middle ages, political or religious as it went off to conquer nations, demanding allegiance at the end of a sword? These beasts have the same effect no matter what clothes they wear.

Those who belong to and worship the beast are marked by him. They wear his mark. But you *cannot* read 13:16 without reading 14:1.

> He also forced everyone, small and great, rich and poor, free and slave, to receive a mark on his right hand or on his forehead, so that no one could buy or sell unless he had *the mark, which is the name of the beast* or the number of his name. This calls for wisdom. If anyone has insight, let him calculate the number of the beast, for it is man's number. His number is 666. Then I looked, and there before me was the Lamb, standing on Mount Zion, and with him 144,000 *who had his name and his Father's name written on their foreheads.* (13:16-14:1, emphasis added)

Why do people make endless speculations about the mark of the beast without thinking about the mark of God? Believers are sealed on their foreheads by God himself, but we don't see a physical mark. We never expect that we will see a physical mark of God, or the name of God, on someone's forehead. So why are people so passionate about finding a physical mark of the beast?

Old Testament Israel made exactly the same mistake. God told the people to have his Word on their wrists, as a frontlet between their eyes, and on the doorposts of their houses. Thinking literally, that is exactly what they did. They made little wooden boxes, put the Word of God in them, and wore them on the wrists and foreheads. We look back on that and smile at their literalist misunderstanding. We know what God meant. But today, every new bar code or credit card is somebody's new "mark of the beast".

Remember, the mark of the beast represents a *spiritual* choice with *eternal* consequences. It is not a matter of being tricked into having a telephone number with 666 in it or buying a packet of cheese that happens to have a bar code!

Make the simple deduction – will someone ever go to hell for eternity because of a credit card? If that could be true, then God need not have sent Jesus, he need only have sent a banker. Don't make the mistake of Israel and become so focused on literal things that you miss the point. The point is that the world is divided into two groups of people and has been since the cross. One group is sealed with the promised Holy Spirit. Its people have the name of God on their foreheads. They carry God's mark of ownership. The other group has the mark of the beast and belongs to his kingdom. The way to go from death to life is to trade one mark, one stamp of ownership, for the other. And we do that by faith in the one who loved us and gave himself for us. No credit card or bar code on earth is capable of undoing or overturning the work of the cross! Don't dishonour Christ with foolishness!

And the number? The book of Revelation is a book of symbols, not a book of riddles! God has not written some sort of children's puzzle book. He has inspired an apocalyptic document whose images last through all time and are appropriate for all cultures. In 13:18, we are not told to work out the puzzle to discover what the mark or the number is. We are told to calculate it, or add it up, and then are told *exactly* what it is. John says, "calculate the number of the beast, for it is the number of *a man*" (RSV, emphasis added). In everything so far, God's number has been seven. This number is six, upon six upon six. This beast is not a god but is always represented as a human being. Hendriksen suggests falling short of seven, and seven and seven is "failure, upon failure, upon failure"[48] to achieve the lordship for which each "world ruler of this present darkness" craves.

Think of the great empires and emperors that people have worshipped throughout history. Or who have demanded to be worshipped. Where now is Nero? Where now is Genghis Khan? Where now is Mao? Where now is Stalin? Where now are the

---

48   Hendriksen: More Than Conquerors, Grand Rapids 1998 p151

unbelieving British kings, American presidents and European dictators? Their bodies rot in graves while their spirits rot in hell. They were worshipped as gods, but are nothing but men.

At a future time, it may be that the whole world will become the same as many individual nations have been. Those who do not have the mark of the beast, do not worship or belong to the kingdoms of this world and will not able to take part in its economic life. As I write this, I am sitting in a country completely closed to the Gospel. I have made notes of the life stories of the group of believers with whom I am having fellowship. In my notes, each believer's story has the phrase "cannot get work because he is a believer". It is a common denominator among them. Their problem is that they do not carry the mark of the beast, but are sealed with the seal of God. Therefore, they are outcasts in the kingdom of this world, cut off from its economy. To look for special marks literally tattooed on foreheads is to miss the point. Tattoos just aren't that clever! Let's stop spooking each other like children telling ghost stories!

Jesus said,

> Do not be afraid of those who kill the body but cannot kill the soul. Rather, be afraid of the One who can destroy both soul and body in hell. (Matthew 10:28)

Concentrate on the fear of the Lord, which is, after all, the beginning of wisdom (Psalm 111:10).

The Third Vision: The Lamb and his followers – chapter 14:1-5

The chapter and verse divisions were not in the original. Therefore, if we read it as one section, without the chapter break, we can see quite clearly what the Spirit of God is doing with the structure. Here are the two branches of humanity: those with the mark of the beast on their foreheads, and now those with the name of the Lamb and his Father on their foreheads. This latter group sings a song that no one can know except them. We will not have to wait until just before the end to be marked as either God's or Satan's. If you have believed in Jesus, you are marked now! You are sealed with his Spirit now! "The Lord knows those who are his" now![49] So too, are those who die rejecting Christ as saviour. Eternal destiny is not determined differently because someone lives in the last days of history. Human destiny is settled on the basis of our faith in Christ, no matter in what era of history we live.

As you look at the group of people who have the mark of God on them, just take a quick glance at our freeway sign again – "Go back. You are going the wrong way" – to make sure you don't step out of the genre. Look at the main, easily determined, aspects of their description:

- They have the name of the Lamb and the Father on them.
- They have been redeemed from the earth.
- They have been purchased as firstfruits for God and the Lamb.
- They sing a new song before the throne.

Who does that sound like? It sounds like the followers of Jesus. Those statements are true of *all* who have believed in the Lord Jesus Christ throughout history, including you. Just as slaves were marked with their owner's mark, you have been marked with God's name. He has entered the slave market and redeemed you (from the earth) as his own. You are also the firstfruits. "Firstfruits" is not a statement of time but of ownership. In Scripture, the "firstfruits" belong to God, which is why Paul used the term

---

[49] 2 Timothy 2:19 Nevertheless, God's solid foundation stands firm, sealed with this inscription: "The Lord knows those who are his."

"firstfruits" to speak of himself and those who had believed in *the first century*. Paul also uses the term of Jesus in 1 Corinthians 15:22-24. It is not a term reserved for a group of people at the end of time (lastfruits?) but for all those who belong to God from the first century onwards.

So who might this group of people be? They are the same numberless throng we met in chapter 7, "with the seal of God on their foreheads" (7:3). It is the believers, as opposed to those with the mark of the kingdom of this world on them.

What are we to make of the additional descriptive phrases? These people are described as not having defiled themselves with women. Can it be that only bachelors who have never had a lustful thought in their entire lives are among the ones who sing the new song in eternity?[50] Can it be that in addition to the blood of Christ, chastity and bachelorhood are the necessary prerequisites for being before the throne? That is what the Roman Catholic Priesthood tried to achieve, with disastrous results! Does this mean that women cannot be a part of the group?

All the way through Scripture, God has used fidelity in marriage as an image of faithfulness to him. In this book, a relationship with Babylon is described in terms of lust and adultery. In the seven letters, we saw "adultery" used to speak of acceptance of the false teachings of the false prophetess. And those of us who love Christ are described as a "bride". These are all images of purity and impurity of spiritual relationships.

God created marriage as good. Marriage and procreation are *not* defilement! It is the first and finest of human relationships, and therefore, right through the Old Testament, its corruption is symbolic of the worst of relationships. It would seem, therefore, that the easiest way to understand its use in an apocalyptic book is

---

50   You might like to remember what Jesus said about lust and adultery in Matthew 5:28, and then calculate how many men would be able to sing the new song!

as an image of spiritual fidelity. These people are also described in terms of truthfulness, and are said to be blameless. These are the people of Jesus, whose lives have been changed by the Gospel.

The Fourth Vision: The angels of grace, doom and warning – chapter 14:6-13

We have seen the rival kingdoms. We have seen the followers of the beast and the followers of the Lamb. We have seen humanity divided into two groups, each with a mark of ownership. We have seen the struggle between the rival kingdoms.

How does this struggle end? What brings history to its close? Obviously this section is not yet complete; we need to be shown how it comes to its final conclusion.

The next section of chapter 14 is a summary that will be expanded in later chapters.

FOURTEEN

The end of the rival kingdoms
Revelation chapter 14:6-20

Chapter 14

The end of the rival kingdoms
Revelation chapter 14:6-20

For the people with the mark of ownership of the beast on them, it must appear to be a hopeless situation. If he has marked them, and that mark seals their eternal destiny, how might they escape? As always, escape is through the Gospel. Never forget that the Gospel is the only hope of rescue.

There are some who teach that in a special seven-year tribulation period, people will be saved by shedding their own blood; their martyrdom securing their salvation. What a disgrace! What a shocking dismantling of the essential sacrifice of Christ! Salvation comes no other way than by the finished and final work of Christ 2,000 years ago.

That is the message that is proclaimed to all nations. While the beasts deceive and woo people's affections towards the dragon, the eternal Gospel continues to be proclaimed.

> Then I saw another angel flying in mid-air, and he had the eternal gospel to proclaim to those who live on the earth – to every nation, tribe, language and people. He said in a loud voice, "Fear God and give him glory, because the hour of his judgment has come. Worship him who made the heavens, the earth, the sea and the springs of water." (Revelation 14:6-7)

It is the eternal message: judgement is coming, the hour is near, fear God and worship him. And alongside that message is the message that Babylon is fallen. What is Babylon? We will see Babylon described in detail in later chapters. For now, were we to simply take the context at face value, we would see that there are two kingdoms at war. One is the kingdom of the dragon, worked out in history through his two beasts, the religious and political empires of this world. The end comes, and those who worship the beast are thrown into eternal torment. Ahead of that eternal judgement comes the proclamation, "Babylon is fallen". The end of Babylon comes with the reaping of the whole earth (verses 14-20). You will note that once again, we have reached the end, or the final judgement. Each time we do, you will see how impossible it is to make this book fit into a linear chronology. As was said in the keys to interpreting Revelation, this book is a series of overlaid visions, each covering the same time period, and each bringing us to the same end (see chapter 3 of this book).

There are only two groups of people being reaped – those who go to life and those who go to death. There are only two marks that determine eternal destiny – the mark of the beast and the mark of God. The people who go to eternal torment are those with the mark of the enemy on them. If something called Babylon "falls", and then eternal torment comes for the people of the beast, Babylon must be the kingdom or structure under which they live. It collapses, and its people are judged. At this point, the simple impression the context gives us is that Babylon is the kingdom these people had embraced, the kingdom of this world.

To make Babylon just one city, empire or organisation, is to divide the world into three – the believers, the unbelievers, and the people of Babylon. That cannot be. We will be able to test this initial impression when the fall of Babylon is expanded in chapters 17 and 18. But where does the name Babylon come from? Why Babylon?

The beginning of Babylon is located in Genesis, where we read of the post-flood people collecting together to defy the plan of God for the earth. After the flood, God had told mankind to spread out across the earth. He had made a new covenant with Noah and his descendants, and they could trust God to provide for them. They were to be his people. But no. "Let us . . . make a name for ourselves and not be scattered over the face of the whole earth."[51] Instead of spreading out across the earth, they gathered in a city called Babel, united by their own arrogance, making a name for themselves. God destroyed their plan by separating them into various languages and people groups.

Since then, time after time, empires have arisen that have wanted to conquer the whole world, to make one world government again: one nation under one ruler, with one language. They have attempted to make a name for themselves, and have compelled everyone to speak the one language again. Babylon, Persia, Rome and on and on ever since. The French did it; the Dutch did it; the British and the Spanish did it. In our own lifetime, the Soviet Union did exactly the same, compelling people to come under their rule, making Russian the universal language.

There will be much more about Babylon later, but here, it is the world system arraigned against God and his Christ. Not just one city but all cities. Not just one empire but all empires. From the beginning, the nations have been made to "drink the maddening wine of her adulteries" (verse 8). But its destruction is sure. In this chapter, we are given a one-verse preview of its fall. It will drink the wine of God's wrath.

The message to the saints is to be patient. The end will come, and God's wrath will be poured out. Just as the deeds of the worshippers of the beast follow them, so will the deeds of believers follow them. The worshippers of the beast will go to torment; the followers of the Lamb will go to an eternity of blessing.

---

51   Genesis 11:4

In verses 14-20, we are once again brought to the end of all things. The reaping of the earth will only ever happen once. It comes as the conclusion of the two kingdoms, the two groups of people, and the two marks of ownership.

In any harvest, what comes first? The firstfruits. That is how we have been described in earlier portions of this book, as well as in the epistles.[52] Following that is the harvest of the unrighteous, gathered into the winepress of God's wrath. The first reaper sits on the cloud and is like the Son of Man. The second is an angel. As we see the harvest of the unrighteous, we realise how terrible the wrath of God is. It is described in human terms, with blood flowing for 300 kilometres as high as a horse's bridle. The images are terrifyingly clear.

Having once again reached the end, a new scene opens before us.

Chapter 15:1-8 has the appearance of a conclusion and also an introduction. We see all of those who did not have the mark of the beast on them. They are in glory, the final reaping having taken them from the earth to be with their Lord. They are singing the songs of Moses and of the Lamb. The song of Moses was a song of victory. That neatly concludes the previous section. However, the section also introduces to us the seven last plagues. There is something else we need to understand. We have seen the flow of history up to the end. We have seen the warnings. What we are now about to see is the wrath of God.

> I saw in heaven another great and marvellous sign: seven angels with the seven last plagues – last, because with them God's wrath is completed. (Revelation 15:1)

---

52   We noted earlier that the term "firstfruits" was ultimately more about ownership than the order of the harvest – the firstfruits belong to God. But in the normal course of events, the firstfruits are indeed the first fruits to be harvested. It is a term with both literal and symbolic meaning.

FIFTEEN

The seven last plagues
Revelation chapter 16:1-21

Chapter 15

The seven last plagues
Revelation chapter 16:1-21

This next scene shows us the bowls of wrath. Throughout Revelation, wrath is associated with the end. The "day of wrath" is the day of final judgement. The use of the word in association with these plagues could be a suggestion to us that what we are about to read is right at the end. That concept is strengthened when we realise that the things we read about in the bowls are the same in nature as what we read about in the trumpets. The difference is in the magnitude of their power and effect. Where the trumpets were warnings to an impenitent earth, the bowls are the wrath of God poured out.

Look through the following chart and notice the similarities between the trumpets and the bowls:

	First	Second	Third	Fourth	Fifth	Sixth	Seventh
Trumpets	Earth 8:7	Sea 8:8	Waters 8:10-11	Sun 8:12	Smoke from Abyss 9:1-11	The great river 9:13-21	The end 11:15-18
Bowls	Earth 16:2	Sea 16:3	Waters 16:4-7	Sun 16:8-9	Throne of the beast 16:10-11	The great river 16:12-16	The end 16:17-21

Just as the trumpets ended in the final judgement, so too do the bowls. Once again, we are taken through a vision that brings us to the end. Once again, we see that this book is not a series of scenes laid end to end chronologically, but a series of overlapping scenes. You will also notice a similarity to the plagues of Egypt. These make them images with which we are familiar. Were we to look back through our Bibles for the most graphic season of the wrath of God poured out upon a nation and the gods they served, it would be the period of the plagues in Egypt. It was a period when the gods of the people were powerless to save them, but also a period when the people of God were spared. It is most fitting that God uses Egypt-type images to speak of his wrath poured out upon all the nations of the earth.

Right through history, when nations and civilisations have come under the direct judgement of God, they have remained hardened in their hearts. Here now, the whole earth faces the plagues, and the whole earth remains unrepentant. With these bowls, the wrath of God comes at the end. When the seventh bowl is poured out, the final judgement comes. There is no more time.

At the beginning of this scene, the "tabernacle of the Testimony" (15:5) ("tent of witness", RSV) in heaven is opened. The tabernacle in the Old Testament was to witness to the presence and holiness of God. It was also the place of mercy. The Ark of the Covenant, the mercy seat and the blood of the sacrifice – these were the familiar elements of the tent. Now the tent is opened, and from the presence of God come seven angels. It is said, in verse 8, that God's presence was shut off from people until his wrath was poured out in full. This action now, this part of God's work in history, closes off his mercy. Just as God is a God of absolute mercy and absolute grace, so he is also a God of absolute holiness and absolute wrath. Those who will not approach him as the God of mercy, will be shut out from him as the God of wrath. Note also, that the bowls are full. The people of earth will now experience the full extent of the wrath of God.

It is for this reason that these bowls appear to speak of the final time, the time just prior to the end. All through history (with the seals and the trumpets), there is a percentage of earth upon which judgement comes. At first it was a fourth (chapter 6:8). With the trumpets, the portion increased to a third (chapter 9:15). But now, with the bowls, the work is total. The wrath of God is no longer mixed with mercy. None escape. All those who have aligned themselves with the beast and the dragon are now irreversibly marked, and face the wrath of God.

The images are graphic and horrifying. As for imagining their literal fulfilment, that is an unnecessary mental exercise. The sea, for example, turning into the blackened, congealed blood of a dead man – is it a literal fulfilment we are being shown? Or are we being told that the sea, a source of so much life, has become death itself. Perhaps the marine environment is so polluted, so unbalanced, that in a final collapse, the entire system shuts down; the oceans, finally and irretrievably lost as a source of life. Would that be sufficient to make us imagine it being the wrath of God poured out on mankind? I think so. And the use of congealed blood of a dead man, as an image of irretrievable death, is so startling, so sickening, as to get under our mental filters and to attack our emotions.[53]

To try and imagine how each will be literally fulfilled will be to waste energy outside the apocalyptic genre. (Do

---

53   I am not for one moment suggesting that God cannot repeat what was done in Egypt on a worldwide scale, filling every ocean with blood. Of course he can! However, I am suggesting that the parallel with Egypt in these plagues is intended as a reminder of the awesome power of God rather than necessarily suggesting a literal fulfilment. Too much time and energy goes into the distraction of trying to imagine what specific disease or event might be coming. The power of the image is then lost in weighing impossibilities in our finite minds. The power of the images lies in the fact that they *are* images. If the images are so graphic, the reality will be unmistakeable in its terror for a fallen, unrepentant world.

you remember in chapter 2 of this book, where we saw how senseless it would be to try to literally define the apocalyptic images in David's song, as he described God as breathing out fire and smoke through his nose, and having burning charcoal in his mouth? Stay with the genre!) The ultimate horror is not a literal ocean filled with congealed blood, but that finally the God of heaven and earth has said, "Enough! Mercy is finished".

And so the voice comes from the temple, "Pour out the wrath."

Bowl 1 – Foul and evil sores. Total and universal misery is inflicted upon mankind, but *only* upon those who have the mark of the beast.

Bowl 2 – Death in the sea. Like the congealed blood of a dead man, irretrievable death comes upon the major source of life for many of the world's people.

Bowl 3 – Death in the rivers and waterways. Blood speaks of death. The people of earth have shed the blood of the saints, and now they too will know death. What judgement they have given they will receive.

> You are just in these judgements, you who are and who were, the Holy One, because you have so judged; for they have shed the blood of your saints and prophets, and you have given them blood to drink as they deserve. (Chapter 16:5-6)

This clearly is an image. Literally drinking blood is not the point! The point is that of sowing and reaping. People deserve what they receive.

Bowl 4 – The scorching of the sun. Everything that formed the normal framework of mankind, and which seemed to make life go on forever, is now turning against man. The sea, the rivers, and now the sun are becoming man's enemies. Creation itself is being turned against mankind. *But* men still do not repent; they merely curse the God who was afflicting them.

BOWL 5 – Here judgement is poured out upon the whole kingdom of the antichrist. In the plagues of ancient times, Egypt was plunged into darkness. Now the whole of the kingdom of this world is plunged into darkness. Again, literal darkness is not necessary. Think of the end of Hitler. If we said about the final stage of the war, "Hitler's troops and the whole German nation were plunged into darkness", would that be a legitimate description? Yes. Would it need to mean that the sun stopped shining? No. In fact it is more powerful because it is *not* literal. If the sun stops shining, you can light a lamp. No lamp on earth was powerful enough to dispel the darkness of Hitler's Germany. Even though the sun continued to shine brightly over the end of the Third Reich, the nation was in darkness and chaos – that is far more powerful than trying to imagine a super eclipse. In the fifth bowl, such darkness will come upon the whole earth.

BOWL 6 – Here we come to the Armageddon. The Israelites thought of all their enemies, and all that was evil, as coming from beyond the Euphrates River: Assyria, Babylonia, and the Medo-Persians – the three great enemies of Israel. And now, in John's vision, the only natural barrier, the river itself, is dried up so that the enemy has no hindrance. The enemy can come and attack. However, stirred up by demonic spirits coming from the dark kingdom, they don't realise they are coming to a trap; they are coming to their own eternal defeat.

"Armageddon" simply means the "Hill of Megiddo", and is first shown to us as a battle ground in Judges 4 and 5. In those chapters, the cruel armies of the Canaanites gathered for battle against Israel. They had been continually persecuting Israel, and now they gathered for a final showdown. But Deborah encouraged the men of Israel by instructing them that the Lord would fight for them. And Israel won, defeating even the generals themselves.

Look at what Deborah said of the battle in Judges 5.

> O LORD, when you went out from Seir, when you marched from the land of Edom, *the earth shook, the heavens poured, the clouds poured down water. The mountains quaked* before the LORD, the One of Sinai, before the LORD, the God of Israel. (Verses 4-5, emphasis added)

> *From the heavens the stars fought,* from their courses they fought against Sisera. *The river Kishon swept them away,* the age-old river, the river Kishon. March on, my soul; be strong! (Verses 20-21, emphasis added)

These are images used to convey the enormity of the work of God. The stars did not actually fight, but we sure get the message!

The hill of Megiddo is now brought back to us as the scene for the final battle. It becomes a symbol of the final battlefield where God's heavenly armies will defeat the demon-led forces of evil. Will all the kings of the earth literally go to the small hill of Megiddo in Palestine to fight against God? How will they all fit, even if we take in the whole region? What weapons will they use to shoot at God? The point is not found in scientific literalism! Stick with the genre. The point is that the enemies of God are now going to act with unity to overthrow the rule of God by destroying the people of God. But it is demonically inspired stupidity. Just as, when Israel was at its weakest, God acted and delivered them, so now, when the church appears poised to be destroyed, God acts to deliver his people.

God brings the end *before they have a chance to act*. It is not a battle between Russia and America. It is not a battle between China and Australia. Not only would none of those battles take place at Megiddo, it is also a fact that the "mythical" battle of Armageddon is never fought! I use the term "mythical" to speak of the ridiculous attempts that have been made to have Armageddon fought over Cuba, or Korea, or 9/11 or any other war between nations and ideologies. This battle, for which the kings gather, is in fact the defeat of *all* kings and *all* nations of the *entire* earth, at the hand of God himself. There are no guns and bombs! With a word he declares the end.

Please, let's stop scaring each other half to death with spooky threats about World War III or any other war! There may be a World War III, but it will not be Armageddon, because World War III would not be a united world fighting against God. It would be nations fighting against other nations. The enemy, that ancient serpent, always wants to deflect our attention away from God himself and place it onto man. Every scary Armageddon threat raised by end-time gurus has done just that. It has made us think Russia, or China, or America is the perpetrator of the final battle and that we will get caught up in a war. The terrifying reality for the people of the earth is that the enemy is none other than God himself! And you cannot shoot him with a gun, bow and arrow, or nuclear missile.

> The seventh angel poured out his bowl into the air, and out of the temple came a loud voice from the throne, saying, *"It is done!"* Then there came flashes of lightning, rumblings, peals of thunder and a severe earthquake. No earthquake like it has ever occurred since man has been on earth, so tremendous was the quake. The great city split into three parts, and the cities of the nations collapsed. God remembered Babylon the Great and gave her the cup filled with the wine of the fury of his wrath. *Every island fled away and the mountains could not be found.* From the sky huge hailstones of about a hundred pounds each fell upon men. And they cursed God on account of the plague of hail, because the plague was so terrible. (Chapter 16:17-21, emphasis added)

This is the third time we have read of every island fleeing away and the mountains being destroyed. May I once again remind you that the end of all things does not come three times? Or five, or six or seven? As we have noted many times – and by now it should be obvious from the flow of the book – Revelation is a series of parallel visions, each of which brings us to the end of history. This time, the focus has been on the wrath of God, which seems to be poured out upon the earth in a period just before the end. It encompasses all the earth. It leads to the final destruction of the kings and nations of the earth.

And once again we meet Babylon, the great city that is the kingdom of this world. With all of its seductive influences, all of its vices and religious harlotries, it is crushed, never to rise again. It falls apart, splits into three, and is made to drink the cup of God's wrath. "Three"? Perhaps because of the three demons mentioned, simply showing that, as is the evil, so comes judgement.

The people of earth are "stoned" to death, with huge hailstones[54] from heaven, by the hand of God himself. The one who is without sin has indeed cast the first and the final stones.

But how does Babylon fall? That is the subject of the next vision.

---

54 It is not possible to read the Old Testament without seeing that fire, sulphur, earthquakes, hail, floods, lightning and other natural elements and calamities are used to speak of the judgement of God. We see it in the prophets, the history books and the Psalms. In Egypt, the plagues were real. From then on, mostly (but not always) these elements are *symbolic* of his wrath poured out. We see this in Deborah's song, David's song, and many other places. Stay with the genre!

SIXTEEN

The fall of Babylon
Revelation chapters 17:1 to 19:8

Chapter 16

The fall of Babylon
Revelation chapters 17:1 to 19:8

In chapter 14:8, we have heard the cry, "Fallen is Babylon". Then in 16:19, we have been told of the total collapse of the city. But as yet, we have no real details of her character or of her destruction. It is here in chapters 17 to 19 that we are shown those details. At the risk of overkill, let me say again that this indicates the impossibility of reading Revelation as a sequence of chronological events told in advance. Babylon is already destroyed (chapter 14), now we read of her destruction. Therefore, since she is already destroyed, it is impossible for the timing of chapters 17-19 to come after chapters 14-16. No, these chapters give us another view, overlaid upon what has already been shown to us. Why did the Spirit inspire John to write this way? Perhaps there is too much for us to take in all at once, so each scene focuses our attention on another aspect of God's work. Each new scene answers another question, or series of questions, for us. In this case, the questions to be answered are: who exactly is Babylon, and how does she fall?

The section is written as the blending of two images, or two major figures, both of which are finally seen to be the one horrible entity. We have the city, Babylon the great, and we have the harlot. They seem to be described differently but also seem to be the same. By the end of the chapter, we realise that they *are* the same: "The woman you saw is the great city that rules over the kings of the earth" (chapter 17:18).

The woman is the city; the city is the woman. There is no distinction between the kingdoms of the world and the great prostitute. To understand who is who, we need to look at the chapters systematically and put them into their widest possible Biblical context.

As we noted earlier, Babylon as a world system commenced at Babel when humanity exalted itself against the command of God. Instead of spreading out across the world as God commanded, post-flood humanity collected together and built a city and a tower. Instead of finding their security and purpose in obedience to the command of God, they set upon their own idea for creating security. (These events are recorded in Genesis 11.) Ever since, mankind has found security in cities and large numbers, not in the God who made them.

Just a chapter later, in Genesis 12, we see another world system emerge. There we read of God saying to Abram, "I will make a name for you" (Genesis 12:2). This is in direct contrast to the people of the earth who decided to make a name for themselves. And that is where the two world systems emerged and diverged. One group of humanity established a system based upon human pride, ingenuity and self-constructed security. The other became a nation under God, his people, secure in his promises alone. The people of Babel were scattered, but Babylon lived on as a world system exalted against God. Throughout history, successive generations have sought to make a name for themselves, gathering humanity back into one empire, usually by force. The world is littered with the graves of the millions whose lives were subservient to those grand imperial ideals. Babylon represents all that is encompassed by the world system, utterly callous towards its people and their wellbeing, while furthering the murderous destruction of the ancient serpent. It is the pride and vanity of mankind making a name for itself, pleasing themselves, exalting themselves and their own desires and pleasures above God, and yet all the while remaining a puppet of an unseen master.

> As for you, you were dead in your transgressions and sins, in which you used to live when you followed the ways of this world and of the ruler of the kingdom of the air, the spirit who is now at work in those who are disobedient. (Ephesians 2:1-2)

It is that system which provides pleasure and security for fallen humanity, independent of God. It is organised human vanity. It is everything in the world that seduces people away from God and the realities of life in God's world. It encompasses everything that attempts to provide security outside a relationship with our Creator.

In earlier chapters of this book, we saw that the world system is not just political, it is religious. It seduces by appealing to the religious, material and political power-seeking vanities of mankind. Lenin was a politician who became an object of worship. Was his kingdom religious or political? Is Rome a religion[55] or a world political power? Where is the line drawn? Is the great American dream and the worship of democracy a political system or a religion? When does patriotism become religion? When does religion, like Islam, or Orthodoxy become patriotism?

The harlot is the city is the beast is the system . . .

---

55   This comment in no way disputes the sincerity of any Roman Catholic men and women who sincerely seek to follow Christ, but rather denotes a system that, over the millennia, sought to dominate, asserting itself above the reigning monarchs of the time, as did some Protestant systems. Its history, as a system, is one of bloodshed and corruption; however, the history of many of its people has been one of devotion to God and compassion for the poor. Ultimately, the judgement we all face before the throne will be based on one core issue – our relationship with God, established by trusting in Christ alone.

The apostle John said to us,

> Do not love the world or anything in the world. If anyone loves the world, love for the Father is not in them. For everything in the world—the lust of the flesh, the lust of the eyes, and the pride of life—comes not from the Father but from the world. The world and its desires pass away, but whoever does the will of God lives forever. (1 John 2:15-17, emphasis added)

In Revelation, we are about to see the kingdom of this world, typified by Babylon, pass away for all eternity.

The harlot, the great seducer, is seated on the beast. She is riding the beast. Look at her character. She is described as a great prostitute, glittering with gold and precious jewels, drinking filth out of golden vessels; "drunk with the blood of the saints. . . [and] martyrs" (chapter 17:6). This description has often been applied exclusively to specific regimes or organisations. A common view in the evangelical West is that it is Roman Catholicism, but any such exclusively-focused application of the image restricts the illustration too much. Despite whatever prejudices we may have towards any organisation or religious body, this harlot is universal.[56] She touches every nation on earth. She is found wherever Satan clothes himself as an angel of light (2 Corinthians 11:4).

In verse 15, "the waters you saw, where the prostitute sits, are peoples, multitudes, nations, and languages". Do you recall the Kingdom of God, opposed by the harlot and the beast? In chapter

---

56   It is always tempting to view things through our own religious-cultural lens. Yes, we have seen certain religious empires grow to massive proportions, but that does not lessen the impact of local village religions. They too seduce men and women away from God. They too place people into bondage. They too offer to give people the fertility or wealth they desire, just as the Baals did in Canaanite history. Is this or that false religion the harlot? Yes. Is it exclusively the harlot? No. Seduction is seduction, lies are lies, bondage is bondage.

5:9, the Kingdom of God is described as touching every "tribe and language and people and nation". What we are being shown are the great opposites. Throughout history, we have seen the progressive emergence of both Babylon and the line of Abraham – two systems, the lesser set in opposition to the greater. We have the spotless bride of Christ and the great and filthy prostitute. We see the Kingdom of the Lamb and the kingdom of the beast. The mark of God and the mark of the beast.

In Babylon, we have a description of all the religious and political kingdoms of this world. It is not just one false religion but all religions in every nation. To make sure, look at the fall of the great city,

> In her was found the blood of prophets and of the saints, and *of all who have been slain on earth.* (Chapter 18:24, RSV, emphasis added)

Notice the strength of the language. It is not just *all* the saints, and *all* the prophets, but *all who have been killed on the earth.* No matter how much some may want to make Babylon typify any one specific religious system, this city transcends all cities. Prejudice does not create accurate interpretation[57]. The problem is not the overstatement about one false religion; it is that by overstating one false religion, we necessarily understate all the others. If we brand one false religion as the harlot, what does it do to all the others? Are they any less a gateway to hell, or a seductive prison created to deceive the people of the earth? Is the village longhouse, with its idols of fertility and torturous initiation rituals, any less a

---

57 I am not implying the legitimacy or illegitimacy of ascribing "harlot status" to any specific organisation. Rather I am questioning the validity of ascribing *exclusive* "harlot status" to any one organisation, for in doing so, every other anti-Christian, or anti-Gospel regime is excluded. Clearly, many religions and political systems have been guilty of seducing mankind, destroying all who oppose them, and persecuting the saints. And no one city, or system, can possibly be responsible for the blood of "all who have been killed on the earth".

seductive deception of the ancient serpent because it is localised? Are its worshippers any less bound? No, this harlot, this city, is all of the false religions, and all of the false ideologies of the earth. As we have seen in chapter 13, they *all* go back to the same source. Whether they are religious or political, whether they span nations or are concentrated in one village, they ultimately cause men and women to worship the beast and have the number of his name on them.

What about the seven hills? Doesn't that indicate Rome? As you think about that, note that the seven heads are not just seven hills, they are also seven kings. In other words, it is not just (or even) geographical, it is political. It is not just nations within borders; it is political empires that can stretch way beyond borders. It was certainly Rome in John's day, a political system that demanded religious worship – "Caesar is Lord . . ." But in verse 15, we read that the great harlot, Babylon, is *not* just seated on the seven hills of Rome, but on *every nation of the earth*. Again, this city utterly transcends Rome and encompasses all nations.

One of our dilemmas in interpreting this section is to know whether it speaks of a long distant future, or was a coded description for the original readers of the Roman Empire and its various despotic rulers who meted out such persecution upon the saints. Most see it as being primarily a description of past and future empires comprising the flow of history.

In the "five who have fallen", some might see the five great empires dating from Israel's beginning: Old (original) Babylonia, Assyria, New Babylonia, Medo-Persia and Greco-Macedonia. The one that "now is" would be Rome, as if the writer is saying in code, "just like Rome today". According to this view, the one that "is to come" will be all that follows on from Rome, the great developing world empires that have been slowly moving towards one world empire and culture. In the time of John, the Kingdom of God, the rock not cut by human hands (Daniel 2), was already becoming "a huge mountain and fill[ing] the whole earth". This Kingdom of God, of which Daniel spoke, is a worldwide kingdom, touching people from every nation. As God's universal Kingdom, it is universally opposed by every tribe and tongue and nation.

Therefore, the seventh may well be an agglomeration of all of the empires of history since the resurrection, united in the flow of history by their opposition to Christ. These will be followed by an eighth beast (kingdom, as in Daniel) to whom the ten kings belong.

Throughout history, all manifestations of the kingdom of this world are related to the beast and draw their power from it, but perhaps we are being told that this eighth will be the one worldwide embodiment of that kingdom; one final confederated empire to fight against the Lamb. The spirit of antichrist that was abroad in John's own day (1 John 4:3) may finally unite the empires of the world.

Ten may well be a symbolic number, as have been other numbers in this book. We don't need to look for a specific ten.[58] However, if God does show us clearly how these things unfold, we will be grateful for the clarity. But we know enough. We know that "the kings of the whole world" gather for the battle "on the great day of God Almighty" (chapter 16:14). Of these, there are far more than ten!

So yes, perhaps in the five who have fallen we see the great empires leading up to the time the deathblow was meted out to them on the cross. Rome, the seven-hilled city, was the centre of

---

58   In my earlier years, the "ten" was going to be the European Common Market, the so-called treaty of Rome. But the numbers of nations in the united Europe has surpassed that number again and again. And once again, those who would limit our focus by speculating on the details organisations, have made fools of us all but have not apologised for misleading us. Stay with the genre! To know that the empires of this world rise against the empire of the Lamb is enough. Whether they are a literal ten or indeed, ten times ten nations, combined against Jesus and his people, for us the certainty is that Jesus wins!

the world empire at that time. But others would come. Perhaps as we move closer to the end, another great empire will emerge. But in these chapters, God is focussing our attention on the destruction of the harlot and the city of the beast. *That* is the point of the chapters.

The question is not which president happens to be in control or which church is being referred to. The chapters answer the one basic question: What happens to Babylon?

The answer is that she falls, headless, never to rise again. All who committed adultery with her, worshipping her instead of the true King, will suffer with her. Her political and religious empires crumble. The ten horns will begin to hate the very system to which they have given allegiance. They will self-destruct, eating the flesh of the system which spawned them and fed them. But too late, too late, too late – for their end has come. None who worshipped her can look to her for refuge. She is gone!

When these things were read to John's first century hearers, they were not busy plotting and scheming to discover which king was which. They were besieged by the forces of darkness. They were suffering terribly under the mighty hand of the Roman Empire. But God had a message for them: their blood may be shed, but they will rest under the altar until, eventually, they witness the utter destruction of Babylon, cast like a millstone into the sea, never to be retrieved again. Ultimately, Babylon cannot stand against the Lamb, for he is the King of Kings and Lord of Lords. The believers in Uganda, or Rwanda, or Iraq, or Sudan, or Niger, or Turkmenistan, or any other nation, don't have to be thinking about which king is which, and which city is on seven hills. These are thoroughly Western preoccupations! The citizens of those beleaguered, anti-Gospel states need to know just one thing – Babylon falls!

The announcement is now made – Babylon is fallen. What once promised everything has now been shown to be empty and devoid of life. Below the surface of what appeared so beautiful and so powerful, the glittering kingdom of this world, is simply a haunt of evil spirits and demons. Her sins piled up to heaven, and God remembered. She is a proud queen thrown down into the dust.

Note that there is a warning to God's people: "Come out of her . . . [don't associate with her] lest you take part in her sins" (chapter 18:4). Here is a Gospel call, a call of grace, even as the warning of judgement is given.

Every group on earth laments: the kings of the earth, because for them Babylon brought riches and glory and power; the merchants, because for them also it brought riches and worldly goods, uniting the world by commerce, but also trading in the bodies and souls of men (chapter 18:13); shipmasters and sailors, for they made their living from her, tying her empires together with trade.

The saints and prophets have been slaughtered across the entire world, in every land, in every period of history, for the sake of Christ. Babylon is the universal city, the universal organised system of this world that exalts itself against Christ, and through whom the ancient serpent wages war against the other offspring of the woman (chapter 12:17). This evil city shed the blood of the saints and the prophets, and every other human being who died of unnatural causes. Now let *her* blood be shed.

But heaven rejoices. And in a final outpouring of wrath, like a millstone thrown into the sea by a strong angel, Babylon will be wiped from the earth. All that has exalted itself against the God of heaven, all that has anchored itself to this world, will be uprooted and thrown down. Utterly wiped out. Why?

1. Because Salvation belongs to God.

2. Because God's judgements are just. He has not turned a blind eye to Babylon, nor has he forgotten. God's timing has been perfect. Justice has been done, and vindication has been brought for the people of God.

3. Because God reigns. It may have seemed, at times, as if the powers of darkness reigned – the dragon, the beasts, or the kings of the earth in Babylon. But God has reigned all along and the earth and the universe were simply awaiting his timing. Just as, in the Old Testament, Canaan waited in ignorance and arrogance until its wickedness was complete, so too will the earth. God reigns.

4. Because the marriage supper of the Lamb has come. The Bride is ready, dressed in pure white linen. She is righteous and pure, as a Bride of the Lamb should be.

At this point, another question may occur to us: Under whose specific hand does Babylon fall? Who brings it about? The next vision shows us the one to whom all authority has been given in heaven and on earth. We see the ultimate triumph of the Lamb who is the Lion.

SEVENTEEN

The King rides to victory
Revelation chapter 19:11-21

Chapter 17

The King rides to victory
Revelation chapter 19:11-21

A new and glorious scene now begins with the words, "Then I saw heaven opened" (chapter 19:11). After having our vision filled with the harlot and the beast in the last section, this new scene is like manna to our souls. Immediately filling the whole scene is the rider on the white horse. This is the moment we have all waited for. Throughout the book, our anticipation has been building. We have been forewarned of the day when the kings of the earth, and people of every level, will cry out in anguish at the sight of the Lamb (chapter 6). And now, we see him.

In all of our Christian literature, there can be nothing more majestic, nothing more stirring than the sight before us now. If this book and its images have touched the depths of your soul, you are ready for what now fills the screen. The earth has been rocked by bloodshed, war and famine. Empires have come and gone in showers of blood. The saints have been oppressed by the ancient serpent through the empires that he manipulates. At times, the darkness has been palpable. But now, here *he* is! He is breathtaking in his power and majesty. (I have changed the formatting for emphasis.)

I saw heaven standing open and there before me was a white horse, whose rider is called Faithful and True.

With justice he judges and makes war.

His eyes are like blazing fire, and on his head are many crowns.

He has a name written on him that no one knows but he himself.

He is dressed in a robe dipped in blood,

and his name is the Word of God.

The armies of heaven were following him, riding on white horses and dressed in fine linen, white and clean.

Coming out of his mouth is a sharp sword with which to strike down the nations. "He will rule them with an iron sceptre."

He treads the winepress of the fury of the wrath of God Almighty.

On his robe and on his thigh he has this name written: KING OF KINGS AND LORD OF LORDS. (Chapter 19:11-16)

We have read of the kings of earth gathering for the battle in chapter 16:16. All the kings of the earth – what an awesome assembly! Allow them all to run across your mind: America, Britain, France, Australia, Germany, China, Japan . . . Imagine a United Nations summit meeting. Think of the pomp and power, as they determine that they will overthrow, or outlaw, any influence that Jesus may have over the nations of the earth. Many individual nations have tried this throughout the millennia, but now they all gather to combine their energies to rid the word of the sect of the Nazarene, and any lingering influence he, or his people, might have. We don't imagine them actually trying to shoot guns at Christ in glory. They are gathered against him, but are reduced to nothing. One word from the Rider utterly annihilates them. With a word from his lips, they are gathered into the winepress of God's wrath and crushed beyond recognition, eternally less than nothing in a lake of fire.

There is no prolonged battle! Indeed, there is no human battle at all! No nuclear bombs, no SAS forces, no air bombardments . . . just a word from the King of Kings, and they are gone. What we see is the majesty and authority of Christ. He is a King with many names. He is called "Faithful" – he has kept his promise to his people. He is called "True" – his judgement is right and just. His name is "Word of God" – he is the final word of God to fallen mankind. He also has a name that no one knows. And he is named "King of Kings and Lord of Lords". One word from him and Babylon has fallen, forever! Don't fear the mythical Armageddon of the populist literature. Fear him who with a word can bring utter destruction upon the nations of the entire earth!

We don't need to imagine God letting bodies lie around to be eaten by birds, any more than we need to imagine Jesus on a horse with a sword for a tongue. We get the point of all these images without having to try to work them out. In the culture of the Old Testament (and some Middle Eastern cultures today) the ultimate insult of death was to lay unburied on the ground. That is why to hang on a tree was such a curse, because the birds of the air would come and feed on the bodies. Not even the dignity of secret decay, but full public exposure in the process of ultimate degradation, as the body decays into a putrefying mass. And now all of the kings, all of the generals, all of the mighty men, all of the horses and all of their riders, and every man, woman and child is described in those terms of ultimate insult, ultimate dishonour and shame. All humanity, great and small, is destroyed. Once again, we have reached the final moment of history, but this time we are shown it in terms of the triumph of Christ over all his enemies.

While we might rejoice in the victory of the King, also take a moment to ponder the awesome nature of what we see. There is a total absence of mercy! They die; they go to judgement; and then to the second death.

The beast and the false prophet are captured and thrown into the lake of fire. These are the earthly manifestations of Satan's power, and they are utterly destroyed.

What did John see next? Remember, that is the question – not what happened next in a chronological line. As we have seen all the way through, this book is not a chronological line. What he sees next answers the remaining great question: What happens to the serpent? We have seen the beasts destroyed, and all of unbelieving mankind come to its inglorious and humiliating end. But what about Satan? That is the subject of the next section.

EIGHTEEN

The end of the serpent
Revelation chapter 20

Chapter 18

The end of the serpent
Revelation chapter 20

At the beginning of Scripture we meet the serpent, the one who deceives mankind and corrupts all that God made good. We have seen his vicious campaign against the people of God throughout the Old and New Testaments. In Revelation, we have been made aware of the nature of his ongoing campaign against the saints and his deception of the people of earth. And now it is his time! His end has come!

There are two main characters in this section – Satan and the collective body of the saints. And by seeing what happens to the saints, we are shown that the great serpent that many feared so much, is powerless to act unless he is permitted to by the One who sits on the throne. All of his destructive power levelled against the saints does nothing but usher them into their glorious inheritance. Yes, the doorway to our eternal home might be painful – it has been for so many of our brothers and sisters – but on the other side of that doorway is an eternity in which every sorrow and pain is wiped away.

The first thing we read is about in this section is the binding of Satan. He is bound "for a thousand years" and then loosed for a little while. It should not surprise us that Jesus has already made a comment on this, because so much of this book draws on what has been said in other portions of Scripture.

What Jesus said

In Matthew 12:22-32 (see also Mark 3:20-30), Jesus, as the King, was demonstrating his Kingdom authority. He cast out one of the enemy soldiers (demons), removing him without even the hint of a battle. But there were people in Jesus' day who saw him cast out demons and said that it was by the power of Satan. So Jesus told them *exactly* what was happening.

> Then they brought him a demon-possessed man who was blind and mute, and Jesus healed him, so that he could both talk and see. All the people were astonished and said, "Could this be the Son of David?"
>
> But when the Pharisees heard this, they said, "It is only by Beelzebub, the prince of demons, that this fellow drives out demons."
>
> Jesus knew their thoughts and said to them, "Every kingdom divided against itself will be ruined, and every city or household divided against itself will not stand. If Satan drives out Satan, he is divided against himself. How then can his kingdom stand? And if I drive out demons by Beelzebub, by whom do your people drive them out? So then, they will be your judges.
>
> "But if I drive out demons by the Spirit of God, then the kingdom of God has come upon you.
>
> Or again, how can anyone enter a strong man's house and carry off his possessions unless he first ties up the strong man? Then he can rob his house." (Matthew 12:22-29)

In verse 28, Jesus declares, "the Kingdom of God has come upon you." When? At *that* time, during Jesus' lifetime. It was brought about by the incarnation of Christ – the Kingdom came *because* the King came. The proof of it was that the "strong man" had been bound, and was being robbed, right then and there!

Then he further describes what is happening in verse 29. By the logic of a parable, he proves that he can only do what he does because the "strong man", his ancient enemy, has been rendered powerless. In his words, the strong man is tied up. In the older versions, the strong man is "bound". Paul tells us that,

> Having disarmed the powers and authorities, he made a public spectacle of them, triumphing over them by the cross. (Colossians 2:15)

Disarmed, bound and triumphed over – those are not weak terms. They are fruits of the Gospel now, in our lifetime, because they began in and through the life, death and resurrection of Jesus of Nazareth. The setting free of men and women from demonic possession and oppression was proof positive that the strong man was powerless to prevent the King acting in power and authority. And ever since, from every tribe, every tongue, every people and every nation, the King has been robbing the enemy. My dear reader, believe it! Don't allow the enemy to cause you even a hint of defeatism, or any sense of spiritual depression, over the events of this world. Yes, we may well lament the evil and destruction wrought by fallen mankind, manipulated by the great puppet master, but this whole book we call Revelation was written to lift our sights above the evil and to see the victory.[59] If you have

---

[59] The question is sometimes asked, "How can it possibly be said that Satan is bound when he wreaks such havoc on the world?" In response, we might consider whether Satan was totally free, or bound when he afflicted Job? Or in any role he may have played in the crucifixion of Jesus? In both cases we see an inferior being, restricted by a sovereign God, and only able to achieve exactly what God had determined would take place. The point is not that he is without movement, or denied access to the people of earth, but that he is unable to prevent what God determines. He often finds himself achieving God's own purposes and desires. For example, see Acts 4:23-30. If we assume the complicity of Satan in these events, (Jesus spoke of Satan coming for him, see John 14:30-

believed, you are one of those whose names are eternally and indelibly written in the Lamb's book of life. You have his mark upon you. You will appear in white. And there are millions, upon millions, upon millions who share the same glorious salvation.

Sharing in the victory of Jesus

I spend considerable time in countries closed to the Gospel, whose governments' energy goes into the prevention of any mention of the name of Jesus, and there I meet brothers and sisters in Christ. Try as they might, the governments of this world *cannot* prevent the King gathering in his people. The strong man is being robbed day by day, and every day. Satan is powerless to consummate his ultimate revenge or to accomplish his determined objective. That is why he is angry, as we have seen in early chapters of Revelation, and wages war against the saints.

Jesus spoke of the casting down of Satan as a past tense event.

> The seventy-two returned with joy and said, "Lord, even the demons submit to us in your name." He replied, *"I saw Satan fall like lightning from heaven.* I have given you authority to trample on snakes and scorpions and to overcome all the power of the enemy; nothing will harm you. However, do not rejoice that the spirits submit to you, but rejoice that your names are written in heaven." (Luke 10:17-20, emphasis added)

Haven't we read in Revelation 12 that, having been unable to destroy the Child, Satan was cast out of heaven? He has lost every claim to authority and to any place in the heavenly

---

31) we see Satan achieving everything God had predetermined. A secondary consideration is that we ascribe too much direct power to Satan, when, in reality, much of the pain and misery on the earth is brought about by human beings.

realms. Yes, throughout this book, we have seen him deceive, destroy, manipulate and pull strings behind the scenes, but he is *not* able to overcome the Lamb or his followers. He is *not* able to prevent the Gospel of the Kingdom being preached to all nations, as Jesus said it would be, before the end comes. The elect *are* gathered in. The followers of the Lamb *are* marked with the mark of God. They *are* destined for eternity, harvested from the earth, saved from wrath and made spotless for their beloved bridegroom.

Jesus' Kingdom never was of this world. He has told us this clearly and unmistakably (John 18:36). It never was a sanctification of the powers and government structures of this world. The true throne of David upon which Messiah would reign would be on the true Mount Zion. The earthly city of Jerusalem and the earthly Zion were only ever shadows of the heavenly reality. What the serpent thinks he achieves here on earth, can never overturn what has been decreed and established in eternity.

In the passage before us, verses 4-6, John saw thrones. Where are the thrones? The answer is determined quite simply by looking at what else John sees. He sees "the souls of those who have been beheaded because of their testimony about Jesus" (chapter 20:4). Not bodies, but souls.

And as you think about this issue, stay with the genre. Decapitation is not the ticket into an exclusive group of believers. Heaven is not divided into the beheaded and non-beheaded. The image is of martyrdom and is necessary to show the contrast between the work of Satan and the work of God. Satan kills bodies; God gives eternal life to souls.[60]

---

60   I am not in any sense implying that Satan has free reign to destroy the bodies of believers. He cannot act outside the sovereign purposes of God! The point is rather that the worst of his work in relation to believers concerns their mortal life. Satan cannot wreak eternal destruction on those to whom God has granted eternal life. Every martyr for Christ has suffered in the body, but entered a victorious eternity.

What we are being shown in this section is the humiliation and end of Satan. Where are these souls? They are in heaven, the only place where the souls of the believers rest. Where do slain believers "come to life"? In heaven, not on earth. So where is John looking? Into heaven. The thrones John sees are in heaven, and that is where the thousand year reign is based. It is from heaven that judgement emanates.

It is said of these martyred believers that they had died but had come to life and reigned a thousand years. It is also said that this is the first resurrection. Having died they live, and (verse 6) the second death cannot touch them. They are priests of God. Who does that describe? Who dies and comes to life and reigns with Christ? All believers, not just a special group of believers.

Please note that verse 4 does not tell us that they reigned on earth. It tells us that they died but came to life and reigned with Christ a thousand years. As noted above, where do slain believers come to life? On earth or in heaven? This is exactly what Jesus told Martha:

> I am the resurrection and the life; he who believes in me, though he die, yet shall he live; and whoever lives and believes in me will never die. (John 11:25-26, RSV)

Physical death will be followed by eternal life. These martyred saints come to life in the presence of their risen Lord. Where was Jesus when James was beheaded? Where was Jesus when Paul was put to death, or when the believers were burned alive in Nero's garden? Where was Jesus when the saints throughout the ages were burned alive, crucified, fed to wild beasts? He was exalted at the right hand of the Father. And where are those martyred saints now? Do you honestly believe that they are anywhere other than reigning with Christ?

That is the point of this section and the message of this book. Not only has Jesus won the victory, we *share* in that victory for all eternity. Satan can rage and rant and fume and foam and do his utmost to destroy bodies, but he cannot, cannot, *cannot* destroy those to whom God has given eternal life. He may wage war on the offspring of the woman and push them through a painful doorway into eternity, but they go to victory not defeat. He may well think he reigns, but he is a defeated foe, bound, unable to prevent the King gathering people from every tribe and tongue and people and nation. Satan is being plundered every day of every year, in every country, on every continent on earth.

Take care! As we noted earlier, Old Testament Israel missed its Messiah because it wanted an earthly king who would defeat the Romans. Far too many believers are missing what Messiah is doing now because they, too, are looking for an earthly king to reign on earth over an earthly kingdom. They want to see the nations cower at their feet in some future time, and in doing so they miss the wonder and majesty of what is happening now as we pray, and men and women are redeemed in answer to our prayers. And when we die, we are ushered into an eternity that will not be interrupted by a second stint on an earth that will once again reject its King.

Christ is reigning now. Our fallen comrades are alive now. The rest of the dead do not come to life until after the period of the "thousand years". Believers share in the first resurrection, the unbelievers do not. The unbelievers are touched by the second death, the believers are not.

Why a thousand years? Stay with the genre. No other numbers in this book have been scientific, they have been images. All the way through this book, the period of earth is measured in days or a few short years. But these saints are now in eternity, outside time. The passage of years and the effects of the kingdom of this world no longer touch them. They reign for a thousand years – a big number for the Greeks, like a "million" is for us.

Deceiving the nations

And at the end of the thousand years, Satan is released briefly. As we have seen in earlier sections of Revelation, there appears to be the briefest of times, just before the end, when the enemies of Christ appear to have gained the victory over him through the defeat of his people. For two thousand earth-years the empires of this world have been in disarray and disunity. Many kings, many queens, many statesmen have tried to unite nations under one great empire, but always there has been the same broken brotherhood that has divided fallen humanity since Babel. Suspicion and racism, created by language barriers and skin colour, have always prevented the people of the world uniting. At Babel, all the people of earth were deceived into thinking they could create security and make a name for themselves without God, but they lost their unity as a direct judgement of God. Until today, Satan has not been able to recreate that unity. But it appears that, at the end, Satan is given power to lure the nations of the earth into a unity that outstrips anything that has ever happened before. Power in solidarity! Power to finally overthrow the narrow, restrictive, offensive, incorrigible followers of Jesus. Presidents and dictators combine to finally rid the earth of its conscience.

And they succeed – or so they think. The witnesses are destroyed (chapter 11) – or so they think. But in a moment, the breath of life is breathed back into the people of God, and they rise to heaven. At that very moment, the King rides forth and destroys without mercy those who have rebelled against him. It is done. And Satan himself is thrown into the lake of fire.

If this were chronological

Now let's look back the other way. If, as some teach, the thousand years is the next literal sequence in a chronological line, what does it imply about Jesus and the Gospel? This must always be our benchmark.[61]

Think about what he returns to. In chapter 19:17-21, we have read that all human beings have been destroyed by Christ. Every level of unbelieving humanity has been brought to its final destruction and humiliation, as the birds of the air "eat the flesh of kings, generals, mighty men, of horses and their riders, and the flesh of all people, free and slave, small and great" (chapter 19:18). There is no one left – not one single man, woman or child. In such a literal view of this book, the earth has also been destroyed. Every star has fallen, every mountain and island has been destroyed. The grass has gone, the rivers and springs of water are utterly lifeless, the seas are literally a solid mass of congealed blood, and every living creature in the sea is dead. Not one fish is left to eat and not one man, woman or child is left to eat it.

And, according to such a time-line view, Jesus *then* comes back to reign on a throne in Jerusalem. It would be worth asking, "Over whom and what does Jesus reign?" There are no people left! Please double check that in chapter 19:17-18, and then in verse 21 where we are specifically told that *all* the people of earth have been killed by Jesus himself.

If we treat Revelation as a literal series of chronological events, and accept the popular view that the believers come back with him to reign on earth for a thousand years, the only ones who can possibly be on earth are those who have returned with him from glory. And according to this view, Jesus and his followers will literally be living on this utterly decimated planet. (Remember, it is not yet a new earth.)

---

61   Whether or not you agree with the interpretations of this book, or indeed any other Christian book on any subject, the arbiter of truth will always be the Gospel. Always consider what a view or interpretation does to the finished work of Christ on the cross. True discernment begins with a true and correct understanding of the Gospel.

Think about the nature of his reign. We know the city where he lives, Jerusalem, and presumably therefore, the house or building in which he lives. This is not David, this is Jesus. This not a king, this is the King of Kings and Lord of Lords. This is not a Jewish prince, this is the "Mighty God, Everlasting father, Prince of Peace" (Isaiah 9:6-7). This is not a president of limited vision and wisdom, but the one who is altogether holy, altogether lovely, altogether wise, and infinitely gracious, merciful and powerful.

Not only so, but Jesus is accompanied by probably a billion, maybe several billion, transformed, glorified, sinless immortals – every believer who has ever lived, Old and New Testaments combined. They live in sinless perfection as they work to transform this broken world according to the will of the glorified Lord who is living on earth in Jerusalem. Then, after a thousand years of *his* reign on earth, a rebellion of evil, greater than any before in all of the history of the earth, comes against him. So what sort of King has he been? What sort of peaceful Kingdom can produce more evil and rebellious men than at any other time in history, and have them rise up in a great and utterly evil army against Christ? Far from it being the most successful reign in history, according to this chronological, millennial view, the reign of Jesus appears to be the least successful!

Think about what it says of the redeemed in a scheme, as taught by some, in which the ones on earth are believers, the remainder of the population of earth having been destroyed. It must be the believers who rebel. Or, as some would have it, their children. Jesus has finally taken up David's throne on earth, only to fail to usher in the peace and universality of righteousness that the earth has cried out for. His reign ends in unimaginable bloodshed. Is that what you are looking forward to? Is that what Jesus is like? Do you want to come back to an utterly decimated earth, to have another thousand years of producing children to populate it, only to have it end in greater bloodshed than ever before as you watch your rebellious children destroyed?

These are serious questions, and any scheme of a millennium needs to fit them together to make it conformable to the Gospel and the character of Christ.

Think about the effect on the Gospel. Many suggest that the thousand year, earthly reign is for the benefit of Israel. They suggest that now, without Satan's influence (he has been bound), Israel can see her Messiah face to face, and at last is able to choose. (This concept is taken from Ezekiel 20:34-36.)

But Jesus *did* come; he *did* live among his people. He performed the signs of the Kingdom, and openly fulfilled the role and tasks of Messiah among them. He did this for three years, "face to face", and they rejected him. He rose from the dead, and they rejected him. He ascended to heaven, and they rejected him. Now, according to the millennial view, they have a second chance, not just another three years but a thousand years, in the visible presence of the glorified King of Kings and Lord of Lords. And still they reject. And still the question remains: If all human beings have been destroyed – "all flesh" – where do the Jews come from?

The above is not set out to mock any view, but to raise the questions that need to be resolved for that view to work.

Jesus returns once

What did Jesus tell us?

> At that time the sign of the Son of Man will appear in the sky, and all the nations of the earth will mourn. They will see the Son of Man coming on the clouds of the sky, with power and great glory. And he will send his angels with a loud trumpet call, and they will gather his elect from the four winds, from one end of the heavens to the other. (Matthew 24:30-31 NIV 1984)

Jesus said that he will return *once*. At *that* moment, the nations of earth will see him and mourn. The trumpet will sound *once*. The elect are gathered *once*. And they enter the presence of their Lord. Nowhere else in the New Testament do we read of a thousand years of Christ reigning on earth. Surely something so great, so foundational to so many theological viewpoints, as a thousand years of his personal habitation on earth, would at least have some space allocated to it in his teaching. But no, he is silent. Nowhere in the book of Revelation are we shown a seven year period of tribulation on earth, before which the saints are removed. These things are theories brought to the text, not taken from the text. They are theories that can only begin to be built upon a rejection of the genre, style and structure of the book.

Nor does the book of Revelation lend itself to the view held by some (although less popular now) that the world will get better and better until Jesus finally returns; that the millennium is just a glorious continuation of a much-improved world. It may look good from behind the windows of an air-conditioned Western world where medicine and science have so greatly improved, but what about the rest of the world where men, women and children in their millions starve to death, often because of those very improvements that we, in the Western world, demand? While we in the West suck the life out of their economies in the name of globalism, sipping our coffee and eating farm produce at prices *we* want to pay, the underdeveloped nations bear the deathly brunt of ruined livelihoods because their small farms and fishing businesses are crushed under multinational jackboots. No, the world is not improving – parts of it are, but those parts are decimating the remainder by drawing to themselves the greater portion of the world's resources.

The book of Revelation shows us, in a series of dramatic visions, what Jesus plainly taught us about the flow of history in Matthew 24. The earth will always have its four horsemen riding wild across the earth – war, famine, plague and death. It will always have its megalomaniacs brutalising people in the interests of their obsession with power. It will always have its mega-corporations robbing the poor, forcing them into sweatshops and a hand-to-mouth existence, while their shareholders get richer. It will always have its plagues, whether transmitted by fleas or promiscuity.

When Jesus comes back, once, it will be to end that corruption and bring eternal peace and joy to those who have reached out to him in desperation over their lost souls. He is the Good Shepherd. He will lose none of those who are his but will raise them up at the last day.[62] Not to another round of a thousand years of fallen humanity culminating in worldwide rebellion, but to an eternity in his presence.

That is the overwhelming message of the book – Jesus wins. After Satan has been cast down, John sees all mankind standing before the throne and the books opened for their judgement. The righteous go to life. The wicked join Satan in the lake of fire.

---

[62] John 6:37-40

NINETEEN

Back to the beginning
Revelation chapters 21 and 22

Chapter 19
Back to the beginning
Revelation chapters 21 and 22

In chapter 21, we see the grand consummation of all things. Wave upon wave of wonder passes before our eyes as we see and hear the God of heaven and earth declare that he is about to make all things new. All that was lost in Eden is wonderfully restored and then exceeded beyond measure. We come back to the beginning, back to where we lost our dominion. We come back to the tree of life, to the river, to the abiding presence of God.

The nature of the chapters is such that to try to expound them, to try to focus on the details, is to rob them of their majesty. Reading these chapters is like gazing at a brilliant sunset and trying to make it better by describing light refraction and the role of the human eye in determining colour variation. Those things might be good to know, but there is a time for gazing at the colours.

So it is with this section. The "colours" before us are brilliant, and we need to allow their beauty to soak into us. They come at the end of so much intense information about the kingdoms at war. Indeed, this book has taken us "through the valley of the shadow of death". Its goal has been that we might "fear no evil, for you are with me" [63].

---

63   Psalm 23:4

There *is* pain on this earth. Jesus said,

"If the world hates you, keep in mind that it hated me first. If you belonged to the world, it would love you as its own. As it is, you do not belong to the world, but I have chosen you out of the world. That is why the world hates you." (John 15:18-19)

And we have seen that at work! We have seen the forces of darkness violently oppose the saints, but we have also seen the victor. We have been led through to understanding his ultimate victory over all his enemies, and our triumph in him.

Now, having walked that valley, we have come out into the glorious light of eternity. We now see the fruit of the sufferings of Jesus, and the blessings prepared for us.

I was in a country whose brutal dictatorship was opposed to Christ, teaching a group of believers who were openly persecuted for their faith. For them, life was hard. They had suffered loss. They could not meet openly. They lived under constant threat of arrest, beatings and imprisonment. Some had had friends and loved ones simply disappear, never to be seen again, as the authorities maintained their campaign of intimidation, brutality and terror.

As we came to these chapters in our study, I asked the group to read them out loud, each student taking a turn at reading a few verses, and then passing the reading on to the next person. That way, each would have a turn at reading as we finished off this remarkable book.

The second reader in turn was an elderly lady who led a small, underground house church. She began to read, and just kept reading, and reading and reading . . . until she finished off the whole of chapters 21 and 22. She was totally absorbed into the wonder of what she was reading. She had tears flowing down her cheeks as she read wave upon wave of blessing and triumph. The others of us in the small, secret room were transfixed by her voice as she read.

At that moment, I "heard" these chapters as never before. I also had tears in my eyes, as I felt her sorrow and pain give way to joy.

It made me realise that some portions of Scripture are best not analysed, but enjoyed. I suppose that there is a time for detailed exposition of these two chapters, but having heard them on the lips of a believer whose life may well end in martyrdom, and having seen that tear-stained face look up as she finished reading, apologising for monopolising the reading process, I find it almost unnecessary to even consider any form of detailed analysis. I think the blessing is in the reading, out loud if you can.

Let me suggest that, at this point in your study, you do read the chapters out loud and then come back to the few comments below.

The first thing we are shown is the New Jerusalem. It is dressed like a bride, spotless and beautiful. We have already met the bride in chapter 19. She has now been made ready. And the voice from the throne declares what we have longed for since Adam fell and the gates of the Garden of Eden were shut:

> "Now the dwelling place of God is with men, and he will live with them. They will be his people and God himself will live with them and be their God. He will wipe every tear from their eyes. There will be no more death or mourning or crying or pain, for the old order of things has passed away." (Chapter 21:3-4)

At last, God and Man can dwell together again.

In verse 2 and verses 9-10, we discover that the bride is the city, the New Jerusalem. At last, we understand! The holy city is the bride *and* the people are the bride. That means that the city of God *is* the people of God. The dwelling place of God was never about geography, not even Middle Eastern geography. The work of the Gospel was never connected with an earthly city. God has always been concerned with people. So now, the last Old Testament shadow has dissolved into the brilliant light of the reality that comes through Jesus. Jerusalem, the shadow, is now no more. The reality is the people of God. God dwells in them and among them, *forever*!

Those concepts begin to emerge in the prophets, where God spoke of Zion as being a light to the nations, a city from which the justice and mercy and salvation of God would flow to the nations. Mount Zion would be (metaphorically) the highest mountain on earth, one to which all nations would be drawn.

Here now, we see that concept brought to its grand climax, as the city is the people who, in turn, are the city – the New Jerusalem. Jerusalem, Mount Zion, was a shadow; the reality was to be the people of Jesus.

We would not expect a literal city to come down out of heaven, especially not one 2,200 kilometres high! (That's out where some satellites begin their orbits.) Just as we have not needed to find one literal city in the descriptions of Babylon, neither do we need one literal city in the descriptions of the New Jerusalem. We are looking at two kingdoms through this book, two systems, each one a city. One is opposed to God, one is the people of God; one is a harlot, one is a bride; one is Jerusalem, one is Babylon. We are that bride, we are the city, we are Jerusalem, we are the people of God. That is why there is no temple. "The Lord God Almighty and the Lamb are its temple" (chapter 21:22). The temple, as the dwelling place of God, was a shadow; God now dwells among his people because there is no sin to cause a barrier. Nothing can now prevent God and his people walking together.

There is no sun or moon, for "the Lamb is its lamp". There will be no more tears or sorrow or pain in that "city", for the former things passed away.

These things are spoken of as if they are a foregone conclusion. "It is done" (verse 6). It is a completed event. Finished. Those who overcame (by the blood of the Lamb) will be God's children. Those who have rejected all that is holy and true will enter the lake of fire.

And so we have come back to the beginning. In the following table compare the beginning, in Genesis, with Revelation.

Genesis	Revelation
1:1 God as the starting point	21:6 God as the starting point
1.1 The heavens and the earth	21:1 New heaven and new earth
1:3 Light apart from sun and moon and stars.	22:5 Light without sun and moon
1:26 Man in the image of God ruling or reigning over all the earth	22:5 Man ruling and reigning
2:10 A garden with rivers flowing out of it, watering it	22:1-2 City with river flowing out of it
3:8 God walking with man in the garden	21:3 God dwelling with mankind
3:22 Tree of life with free access	22:2 Tree of life with free access
1-2 A creation	21:5 A new creation
3:14-20 Sorrow, pain and death	21:4 Sorrow pain and death removed
3:22 Access to the tree denied	22:2 Access to the tree restored.
3:24 The gates of the garden shut	21:25 Gates of the city opened and never shut

Everything has been restored. We drink from the river and eat from the tree of life, just as we had done at the beginning. Since the fall, all human history has moved inexorably towards this grand restoration. The centre of it all has been Jesus. He was, and is, eternally God's plan. He is the Lamb and the Lion, the Servant and the King.

The gates of the city carry the names of the twelve tribes of Israel, and its foundations the names of the twelve apostles. The people of God are *one* nation, *one* new man, *one* people. There are not two people groups, Israel and the Gentiles. There has only ever been one people of God, those born according to the promise (Romans 9). We have been brought together as the children of Abraham, the Israel of God (Galatians 3:6-7; 6:15-16).

Jesus has won the victory. His work is done. He most certainly deserves to receive all honour and glory and praise.

The curse remains upon those who have continued to reject the altogether lovely One (chapter 22:11). But for those who long for his return, there is joy forever more. Perhaps, in our hearts, we cry out like those under the altar in chapter 6, "How long?" For us it may seem too long, but when we finally walk through the gates of that city, our history on earth will be like the blink of an eye. The labour pains may be hard, but the result is beyond comprehension.

Epilogue chapter 22:20,21

"I am coming soon."

This is his pledge and promise to us.
So too is his grace with us.

"The grace of the Lord Jesus be with God's people.
Amen." (Verse 21)

A FINAL WORD

From Pilgrim's Progress, by
John Bunyan

A final word

From Pilgrim's Progress, by John Bunyan

The King then commanded to open the gate . . .
Now I saw in my dream, that these two men went in at the gate; and lo, as they entered, they were transfigured, and they had raiment put on that shone like gold. There was also that met them with harps and crowns, and gave them to them - the harps to praise withal, and the crowns in token of honour. Then I heard in my dream that all the bells in the city rang again for joy, and that it was said unto them, "Enter ye into the joy of your Lord."

I also heard the men themselves, that they sang with a loud voice, saying, "Blessing and honour, and glory, and power, be unto him that sitteth upon the throne, and unto the lamb, forever and ever."

Now, just as the gates were opened to let in the men, I looked in after them, and, behold, the City shone like the sun; the streets also were paved with gold, and in them walked many men, with crowns on their heads, palms in their hands, and golden harps to sing praises withal. There were also of them that had wings, and they answered one another without intermission, saying, "Holy, holy, holy, is the Lord." And after that they shut up the gates; which, when I had seen, I wished myself among them.

If you, like John Bunyan, have wished yourself to be among them, there is but one answer. Repent and believe in the Lord Jesus Christ.

As the Lamb of God, he presented himself as the only acceptable offering for your sin. The time to avail yourself of that offering is now. As this book of Revelation has shown, the day will come when everyone will see him, and at that time it will be too late. Your only hope is Jesus. Your secure hope is Jesus.

He *is* Lord; he *has* been enthroned; your knees *will* one day bow before him. Make it today.

Also by Ray Barnett

The Gathering

Why is church such a frustrating, ineffective experience for so many sincere believers?

Why does the church seem to repel the very people that Jesus attracted? Why is it, that for all the dollars spent on buildings, clergy salaries, and denominational hierarchies, the institutional church seems to remain so ineffective and powerless to change our communities, let alone genuinely impact our own lives?

The simple answer is that, for too many centuries, our institutional structures have been based on a lie. We have been sold the notion that the leadership hierarchies, the clergy system, and the auditorium-based cycles of Sunday meetings are what God instructs us to do in Scripture.

Nothing could be further from the truth.

Challenging each of these fallacies, THE GATHERING sets out the Biblical foundation of what God actually does say about being a local church. For believers who are walking away from the suffocations of the past, or who would like to, THE GATHERING lays out a pathway towards a truer, more Biblical model of the local church.

www.raybarnettbooks.com

www.ingramcontent.com/pod-product-compliance
Lightning Source LLC
Chambersburg PA
CBHW021146160426
43194CB00007B/708